GCSE French by RSL

Volume 1: Listening, Speaking

Visit **www.rsleducational.co.uk/frenchaudio** to download:

➢ Audio material for use with the listening papers in this book.

➢ Example oral exam conversations.

This book contains:

➢ **Four listening papers with detailed solutions**.

➢ An **oral (speaking) primer** with advice, marking guidance and analysis of the downloadable sample conversations.

➢ *Steps to a Higher Grade*: How to boost your written and oral responses.

The listening papers are modelled on papers set by all exam boards for their 9-1 GCSE/IGCSE syllabuses, and cover an extensive range of topics. The questions become progressively more challenging in each paper, from 'warm-up' questions to more advanced comprehension exercises.

The papers are accompanied by highly detailed, *teaching* solution pages and mark schemes. These will guide you through the questions, step-by-step – like having a personal tutor alongside you.

When used together with *Volume 2: Reading, Writing, Translation*, this book offers thorough preparation for an excellent performance at GCSE.

How to use this book

When correcting your work, it's a good idea to take notes of any important learning points, as well as your mistakes: this will make your revision easier. If an answer can be improved, it's worthwhile to repeat it, referring to the examples. Where alternative methods and solutions are suggested, it's often useful to try them out – to find out whether they work for you.

You can attempt these papers with or without time limits. Either way, I recommend working though the solution pages carefully, until you fully understand all the advice.

A note on exam boards

These papers are relevant to **all exam boards**. AQA GCSE, Cambridge IGCSE and Edexcel (GCSE and IGCSE) exams require some answers to be written in French and some in English. Therefore, some of the questions in each listening paper ask you to answer in French, and others in English.

I hope you enjoy working through this book.

We are a family business in a competitive marketplace. We are constantly improving and expanding our range, in order to publish ever-better resources for our customers – in particular, families who find that our books offer better value than expensive private tuition.

If you have any feedback or questions, please let us know! You can get in touch through our website at **www.rsleducational.co.uk**, where you can also view our up-to-date range of publications, or by emailing **robert@rsleducational.co.uk**.

If you like this product, please tell your friends and write a review on Amazon!

Also available

- ➤ GCSE French by RSL, Volume 2: Reading, Writing, Translation
- ➤ GCSE Maths by RSL (Non-Calculator: Higher Level)
- ➤ GCSE Spanish by RSL: Volumes 1 and 2
- ➤ GCSE German by RSL: Volumes 1 and 2

- ➤ RSL 11+ Comprehension: Volumes 1 and 2
- ➤ RSL 11+ Comprehension, Multiple Choice: Books 1 and 2
- ➤ RSL 11+ Maths
- ➤ RSL 8+ to 10+ Comprehension
- ➤ RSL 13+ Comprehension

- ➤ **11 Plus Lifeline** (printable Comprehension, Maths, Reasoning and Writing material, including multiple-choice): **www.11pluslifeline.com**

- ➤ **RSL Creative Writing**: several volumes

Table of Contents

GCSE French by RSL, Volume 1: Listening, Speaking (2nd edition)
by Felicity Davidson

Copyright © RSL Educational Ltd 2021

Cover design by Heather Macpherson at Raspberry Creative Type

Image on 11 Plus Lifeline information page © iStockPhoto.com.
Cover images & graphics © Shutterstock.com.

www.rsleducational.co.uk

Topic Guide

The same core topics are tested by all exam boards, sometimes with slightly different titles (and often with a fair bit of crossover between the sub-topics listed below, depending on the board).

Home and Abroad

- ✓ Town and rural life
- ✓ Weather and climate
- ✓ Everyday life and traditions abroad
- ✓ Neighbourhood and region

- ✓ Holidays and tourism
- ✓ Services such as using the phone, bank or post office
- ✓ Travel, transport and directions

Education and Employment

- ✓ School life
- ✓ School routine
- ✓ Childhood

- ✓ Future plans
- ✓ Jobs and careers
- ✓ Ambitions: further study; volunteering

House, Home and Daily Routine

- ✓ Types of home
- ✓ Self, family, friends and relationships

- ✓ Household chores
- ✓ Food and drink

The Modern World and the Environment

- ✓ Technology and information e.g. internet, mobile phones, social media
- ✓ Environmental issues

- ✓ Current affairs and social issues
- ✓ The media e.g. TV, film, newspapers
- ✓ Bringing the world together: events, campaigns and good causes

Social Activities, Fitness and Health

- ✓ Hobbies, pastimes, sports and exercise
- ✓ Shopping and money

- ✓ Celebrations
- ✓ Accidents, injuries and health issues

Listening Paper 1

> *Visit **www.rsleducational.co.uk/frenchaudio** to download the audio file for this paper.*

If you wish to complete this paper in timed conditions, allow 40 minutes plus 5 minutes' reading time.

Instructions

- Use **black** ink or ballpoint pen.
- Answer **all** questions.
- Answer the questions in the spaces provided.
  - *There may be more space than you require.*
- Dictionaries are **not** allowed.

Advice

- You have 5 minutes to read through the paper before the recording starts.
- You will hear each extract twice. You may write at any time during the examination. There will be a pause after each question.
- Read each question **carefully** before attempting it.
- The marks available for each question are given in [square brackets]. These give you an indication of how long to spend on it.
- There is a total of **50 marks** available for this paper.
- Leave time to check your answers at the end, if possible.

Answer ALL questions.

À l'hôtel

Cochez **[X]** la bonne case A, B, C ou D.
Put a cross **[X]** in the correct box, A, B, C or D.

1   Vous arrivez à l'hôtel en France.
           You arrive at the hotel in France.

           Vous êtes à l'accueil. Vous demandez quel type de chambre?
           You are at the hotel reception. What type of room do you ask for?

Exemple:

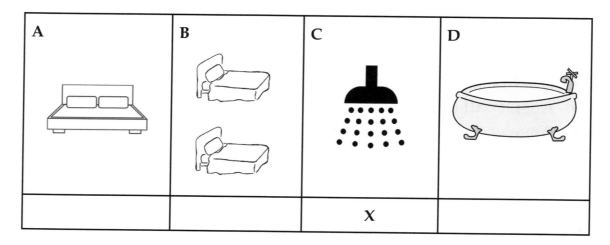

(i)   Vous demandez le numéro de votre chambre. L'employée dit:
            You ask for your room number. The employee says:

A	B	C	D
49	**18**	**89**	**132**

(ii)   Vous demandez à quelle heure le petit déjeuner est servi. L'employée dit:
You ask what time breakfast is. The employee says:

A	B	C	D
08h30	**08h00**	**06h30**	**07h00**

(iii)   Vous êtes dans votre chambre. Où se trouve le code Wifi?
You are in your room. Where is the WIFI code?

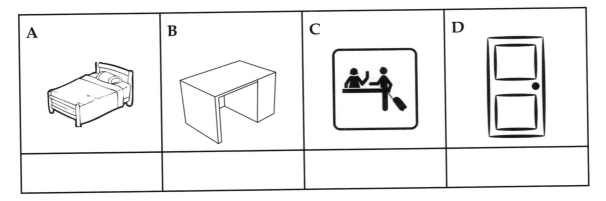

(iv)   Vous demandez où se trouve l'office de tourisme. L'employée dit:
You ask where the tourism office is. The employee says:

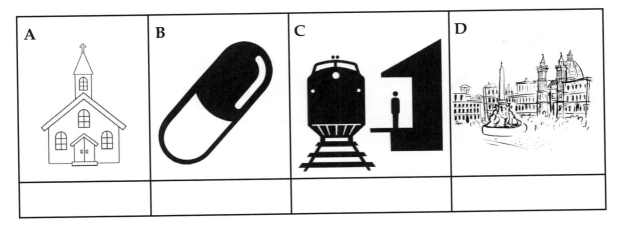

(Total for Question 1 = 4 marks)

La météo

2   Quel temps fera-t-il demain?
     What will the weather be like tomorrow?

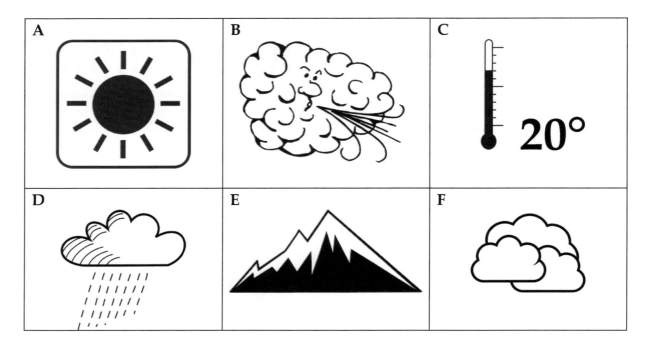

Écrivez la bonne lettre.
Write the correct letter.

Exemple:	C
(i)	
(ii)	
(iii)	

(Total for Question 2 = 3 marks)

La ville

3   Elles vont en ville. Où est-ce qu'elles vont aller?
They are going into town. Where are they going to go?

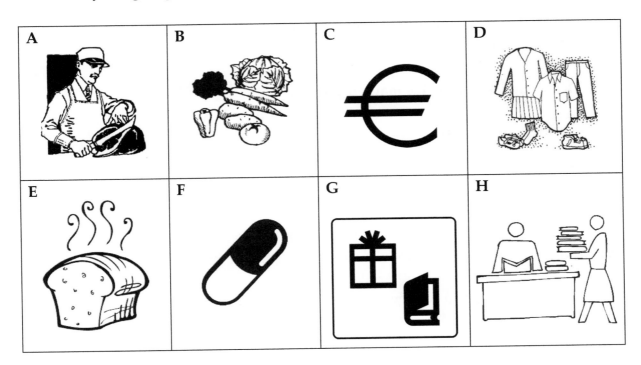

Cochez [**X**] la bonne case.
Put a cross [**X**] in the correct box.

	A	**B**	**C**	**D**	**E**	**F**	**G**	**H**
Exemple:				**X**				
(i)								
(ii)								
(iii)								
(iv)								
(v)								

(Total for Question 3 = 5 marks)

Au collège

4   Tariq parle de son collège. Complétez les phrases suivantes **en français** ou en chiffres.

Tariq is speaking about his school. Complete the following sentences **in French** or using numbers.

Exemple: Matière préférée: <u>**les mathématiques**</u>.

(i)   Nombre de matières: ………………………………

(ii)   Nom de ville: ………………………………

(iii)   Un mot pour décrire son collège: ………………………………..

(iv)   Son trajet au collège dure …………………………….. minutes.

(v)   Heure d'arrivée au collège: ………………………………

(vi)   Mode de transport pour aller au collège: ………………………………

(Total for Question 4 = 6 marks)

Chez moi

5   Que dit Henri?
     What does Henry say?

A utile	B grand	C mauvaise	D loin
E petit	F énervant	G bleue	H blanche
I quatre	J moderne	K cinq	L près
M bonne			

Choisissez le bon mot.
Choose the correct word.

Exemple: Henri habite dans un appartement __moderne__.

(i) Ils ont .... chambres.

(ii) C'est .... d'avoir un garage.

(iii) Leur ancien appartement était ....

(iv) L'appartement est .... de son école.

(v) Sa chambre est ....

(vi) Sa mère pense que la télévision est une .... idée.

(Total for Question 5 = 6 marks)

Les émissions de télévision

6   Que pense Lorraine de ces émissions de télévision?
       Cochez [X] la bonne case.

       What does Lorraine think about these television programmes?
       Put a cross [X] in the correct box.

	A intéressant	B rigolo	C ennuyeux	D passionnant	E effrayant
Exemple: Science-fiction					X
(i) Les comédies					
(ii) Le sport					
(iii) Les séries policières					

(Total for Question 6 = 3 marks)

Les tâches ménagères

7   L'opinion exprimée est-elle positive, négative ou les deux?
    Cochez [X] une case par personne.

    Is the opinion positive, negative or both?
    Put a cross [X] in one box per person.

	☺	☹	☺☹
Exemple:		X	
(i)			
(ii)			
(iii)			
(iv)			

(Total for Question 7 = 4 marks)

Les portables

8   Qu'est-ce qu'ils disent au sujet des téléphones portables?
        Cochez **[X]** les six bonnes cases.

        What do they say about mobile phones?
        Put a **[X]** in the six correct boxes.

Exemple: Christophe pense que les portables sont:

	A	utiles.
	B	énervants.
X	**C**	supers.

(i)   Pendant la journée il…

	A porte son portable sur lui.
	B le met dans un sac.
	C le laisse à la maison.

(ii)   Le soir, il aime...

	A jouer avec son portable.
	B envoyer des emails.
	C parler avec des amis.

(iii)   Jeanne pense que les portables sont...

	A pénibles.
	B utiles.
	C ennuyeux.

(iv)   Quand elle sort entre amis, ses amis…

	A parlent ensemble.
	B partagent des vidéos.
	C sortent sans leur portable.

(v) Maxine préfère quand il a son portable car…

A	elle ne stresse pas du tout.
B	elle peut mieux se détendre.
C	elle ne pense pas à lui.

(vi) Un autre avantage est qu'il…

A	l'appelle tout le temps.
B	a des applications sur son portable.
C	lui apprend à comprendre comment les applications marchent.

(Total for Question 8 = 6 marks)

L'environnement

9   Que dit Aurélie? Cochez [X] les six bonnes cases.
     What does Aurélie say? Put a cross [X] in the six correct boxes.

Aurélie…	
Exemple: …vient de l'île Maurice.	X
A …est venue en France avec sa famille.	
B …est allée en France à l'âge de huit ans.	
C …à habité à l'île Maurice jusqu'à l'âge de dix ans.	
D …a trouvé des problèmes environnementaux en île Maurice.	
E …a vu beaucoup de forêts souffrant de déboisement.	
F …a fait le tri.	
G …ne fait rien pour l'environnement.	
H …n'a pas fait de recyclage.	
I …va à l'école en voiture.	
J …pense qu'il n'y a pas assez de voitures.	
K …aime les transports en commun.	
L …évite d'utiliser les sacs plastiques.	

(Total for Question 9 = 6 marks)

Bien manger

10   Écoutez l'interview et notez les détails **en français**. Il n'est pas nécessaire d'écrire des phrases complètes.

Listen to the interview and write down the details **in French**. It is not necessary to write full sentences.

	Avantages	Inconvénients
Exemple: Être chef	Créer des plats sains	
Manger sainement	(i) (ii)	(iii)
Le petit déjeuner	(iv) (v)	(vi) (vii)

(Total for Question 10 = 7 marks)

TOTAL FOR PAPER = 50 MARKS

Listening Paper 1 – SOLUTIONS

À l'hôtel

1 Vous arrivez à l'hôtel en France **Exemple** *C*	
(i) *A*	[1]
(ii) *C*	[1]
(iii) *B*	[1]
(iv) *B*	[1]

The first questions are always going to involve the easiest vocabulary. This one tests some fairly simple core GCSE words: in particular, numbers, times and prepositions. Normally the title at the top of each section will give you a clue as to what area of vocabulary is being tested – in this case, hotels and holidays.

You are required to put a cross underneath the pictures once you hear the French word(s) in the dialogue. There are **four** marks available for this question. Therefore, you need to cross exactly four boxes.

TOP TIP: Revise numbers!

When you see **numbers,** try to note down what they are in French (e.g. write *quarante neuf* above the large '49') when you go through the paper in your allocated reading time, before the recording begins. This will save you time when listening: especially for difficult numbers in the 80s and 90s such as *quatre-vingt* and *quatre-vingt-dix.*

The recording will play a **second time**, giving you a chance to check and confirm your answers. There will be a short pause after the first recording, and after the second time you hear it.

Below is a transcript, with the key information given **in bold**.

Full transcript for Question 1

Female 1   *Exemple. Je voudrais une chambre **avec une douche***
*Votre chambre est numéro **quarante neuf***
*Le petit déjeuner est servi à **six heures et demie***
*Le code Wifi est **sur le bureau***
*Il se trouve **à côté de la pharmacie***

Mark Scheme:

0-4	- Award one mark for each correct answer, up to four. - If more than one box per question is crossed, then no marks are awarded.

La météo

2 Quels temps fera-t-il demain?	
Exemple *C*	
(i) *A*	[1]
(ii) *F*	[1]
(iii) *D*	[1]

TOP TIP: Revise higher tier topic vocabulary!

Be ready for vocabulary that isn't the most obvious. You may know the following phrases:

Il fait soleil = It's sunny
Il y a des nuages = It's cloudy
Il pleut = It's raining

However, here the answers require higher level vocabulary:

Il fera très beau = It will be sunny
Il ciel sera couvert = The sky will be overcast/cloudy
Un risque d'averses = A risk of showers

Mark Scheme:

0-3	- Award one mark for each correct answer, up to three. - If more than three boxes are crossed, then no marks are awarded.

Full transcript for Question 2

F1 *Bonjour et bienvenue au bulletin météo pour le sud de la France. Ce matin il fait déjà vingt degrés. Il faut aller à la plage aujourd'hui car **il fera très beau** toute la matinée jusqu'à treize heures. Mais à la fin de l'après-midi, **le ciel sera couvert**. Dans le nord-ouest de la France il y aura un risque **d'averses,** alors prenez vos parapluies.*

La ville

---

3 Où est-ce qu'elles vont aller?
Exemple *D*
(i) *A*   [1]
(ii) *G*   [1]
(iii) *E*   [1]
(iv) *B*   [1]
(v) *H*   [1]

It's a good idea to **cross out each picture once you have used it**, so you can see quickly and clearly which ones are left.

Words which sound similar are often used in questions like these, so be careful to learn the difference between *boucherie* and *boulangerie*. *Librairie* and *bibliothèque* are also often used. *Librairie* is a **false friend** and doesn't mean 'library', but 'bookshop'.

Full transcript for Question 3

F2   *Exemple. Demain, je vais aller en ville avec ma mère pour acheter des vêtements.*

F2   *Il me faut du poulet, je vais à **la boucherie.***

F2   *Il y a une nouvelle **librairie** en ville, tu veux y aller?*

F2   *J'ai faim, je vais à **la boulangerie** pour acheter du pain.*

F2   ***L'épicerie** est fermée, quel dommage, je voulais acheter des carottes.*

F2   *Il faut que je travaille, je vais à **la bibliothèque.***

Mark Scheme:

0-5	- Award one mark for each correct answer, up to five.
	- Incorrect or multiple answers score 0 marks for that question.

Au collège

---

4 Tariq parle de son college
Exemple *Les mathématiques*
(i) *neuf matières / 9*   [1]
(ii) *Lyon*   [1]
(iii) *au centre-ville / (très) grand / (assez) moderne*   [1]
(iv) *trente-cinq / 35*   [1]
(v) *sept heures et demie / 7:30*   [1]
(vi) *à pied*   [1]

This is a recording without pauses or multiple-choice options. Try to jot down each answer in the empty space alongside the question when you first hear the recording. When you hear the interview a second time, write your final answers in the spaces provided.

It's useful to **translate key words in the questions** if you can, making use of the reading time at the start of the exam.

Mark Scheme:

0-6	- Award one mark for each correct answer, up to six.
	- Incorrect answers score 0 marks for that question.
	- Only reject if spellings are not intelligible.
	- Grammatical errors will not lose marks

Full transcript for Question 4

F1	*Quelle est ta matière préférée?*
M1	*Ça doit être **les mathématiques**.*
F1	*Combien de matières est-ce que tu étudies?*
M1	*En ce moment il y en a beaucoup, j'étudie **neuf matières**.*
F1	*Où se trouve ton collège?*
M1	*C'est dans le Rhône, dans une ville qui s'appelle **Lyon**.*
F1	*Parle-moi de ton collège.*
M1	*Je l'aime bien. Il est **au centre-ville**; c'est **très grand** et **assez moderne**.*
F1	*Ton trajet au collège dure combien de temps?*
M1	*En général, ça dure **trente-cinq minutes**.*
F1	*Et tu arrives à quelle heure?*
M1	*J'arrive vers **sept heures et demie**.*
F1	*Tu y vas comment?*
M1	*J'y vais **à pied**.*
F1	*Merci beaucoup Tariq.*

Chez moi

5 Que dit Henri?	
Exemple *moderne*	
(i) *quatre*	[1]
(ii) *utile*	[1]
(iii) *petit*	[1]
(iv) *loin*	[1]
(v) *bleue*	[1]
(vi) *mauvaise*	[1]

TOP TIP: Pay attention to the whole sentence.

A common mistake is to stop listening once you think you have heard the right answer: instead, you need to pay attention to the entire sentence in case there are traps.

Be on your guard for additional information, which may contain a word that appears among the options but isn't the answer you're looking for. For instance, Henri says that he has **four** bedrooms (*nous avons quatre chambres*) – but shortly afterwards, he says that it's **five** kilometres from the centre of town (*il se trouve à cinq kilomètres…*). Similarly, he says that their old flat was small but now they are very comfortable, *notre ancien appartement était petit mais maintenant nous sommes très confortables*. The question asks for an adjective for the old flat, so be careful to pick the right adjective (*petit*), and don't be thrown by *confortables*.

Again, with questions like these, it's a good idea to cross off the options you've used. Once you've completed your answers, **check them again**. Make sure you don't have multiple answers for a single question, and that you haven't used the same picture twice.

Full transcript for Question 5

F1   *Henri, vous habitez dans un appartement moderne avec votre famille, n'est-ce pas?*

M1   *Oui, c'est très moderne et nous avons **quatre** chambres. Il se trouve à cinq kilomètres du centre-ville. Nous n'avons pas de grenier mais nous avons un garage qui est **utile**. Notre ancien appartement était **petit** mais maintenant nous sommes très confortables. Le seul inconvénient de notre appartement est qu'il est **loin** de mon école.*

F1   *Votre chambre est **bleue**?*

M1   *Oui, c'est ma couleur préférée. J'ai aussi une télévision dans ma chambre mais ma mère pense que c'est une **mauvaise** idée.*

Mark Scheme:

0-6	- Award one mark for each correct answer, up to six.
	- Incorrect answers score 0 marks for that question.
	- Only reject if spellings are not intelligible.
	- Grammatical errors will not lose marks

Les émissions de télévision

6 Qu'est-ce que Lorraine pense de ces émissions?	
Exemple *E*	
(i) *B*	[1]
(ii) *C*	[1]
(iii) *D*	[1]

Again, this recording is without pauses, so you need to listen attentively throughout and extract the relevant information when it appears. The answers are not always obvious, but they do at least occur in order.

The words Lorraine uses to describe what she thinks of the programs are not the same as the words given in the question under **A**, **B**, **C**, **D** and **E**. This type of question is testing **synonyms**, as 'funny' can be either *drôle*, *rigolo*, *amusant* or *marrant*. Another potential trap is presented here, when ideas are expressed which aren't the **speaker's** opinion. She says that she likes comedies, but goes on to say her sister finds them boring: *elle les trouve ennuyeuses*. The word *ennuyeuses* is an option in the answer, but here it is her sister's opinion, not hers.

Full transcript for Question 6

M1 *Lorraine, quel est ton avis sur les émissions de télévision?*

F1 *Bon, je ne peux pas regarder les émissions de science-fiction, j'en ai trop peur donc je ne les regarde jamais. Les comédies sont bien quand on veut se détendre, mais ma sœur, elle les trouve ennuyeuses. Moi, je pense qu'elles sont **très drôles**. Elle n'a pas de sens de l'humour. Mon frère aime bien le sport, mais **ça ne m'intéresse pas**. Pour moi, les émissions policières sont mes préférées, j'adore les histoires quand il faut deviner qui est le tueur, c'est **palpitant**.*

Mark Scheme:

| 0-3 | - Award one mark for each correct answer, up to three. |
| | - Incorrect answers score 0 marks for that question. |

Les tâches ménagères

---

7 L'opinion exprimée est-elle positive, négative ou les deux?
Exemple (sad)
(i) (happy)   [1]
(ii) (sad)   [1]
(iii) (happy)   [1]
(iv) (both)   [1]

TOP TIP: Make sure to listen to <u>everything</u> each person says, as this may help if you don't know the specific vocabulary.

If you don't know (or can't remember) the meaning of the key word in the recording, **keep listening to the rest of the sentence for clues**. For example, in the first question, the man says that he helps his father prepare dinner, that it's a good time to chat together (*on peut bavarder ensemble*), and that this pleases him (*ça me plaît beaucoup*). If you don't recognize the verb *bavarder* then you still have a chance to get the answer with *ça me plaît*.

Full transcript for Question 7

F1   *Avant d'aller à l'école, je dois ranger ma chambre et ça prend longtemps.*

M1   *J'aide mon père en préparant le dîner, c'est **un bon moment car on peut bavarder ensemble** et **ça me plaît beaucoup**.*

F1   *J'évite de faire la vaisselle car **je me mouille** chaque fois et c'est vraiment **barbant**. En plus, c'est **toujours moi qui dois le faire**.*

M1   *Je déteste le désordre donc moi, je fais tout. Je mets la table et je la débarrasse et puis je passe l'aspirateur. **Ça ne m'énerve pas** parce que **je préfère une pièce propre**!*

F1   *Je dois faire le repassage chaque jour, pour mon uniforme scolaire. **C'est un peu répétitif** mais **ça ne me gêne pas**.*

Mark Scheme:

0-4	- Award one mark for each correct answer, up to four.
	- Incorrect answers score 0 marks for that question.

Les portables

8 Qu'est-ce qu'ils disent au sujet des téléphones portables?	
Exemple *C*	
(i) *C*	[1]
(ii) *C*	[1]
(iii) *A*	[1]
(iv) *B*	[1]
(v) *B*	[1]
(vi) *C*	[1]

Use the pauses between people's statements to make notes and choose your answers. Listen out for synonyms and key phrases, then use your common sense and a process of elimination to arrive at the correct answer.

For the first question, he does say that he has his phone on him almost all the time, but you need to listen to the rest of the section for the key words *malheureusement* and *interdits* to understand that he has to leave his phone at home. Also, watch out for traps in the multiple-choice answers. The second question is looking for the fact that he talks to his friends in the evenings. He mentions that he sends texts, (*j'envoie tous mes textos*) and there is a similar statement in the question, *envoyer des emails*. It's the same **verb**, but the **noun** is different.

Full transcript for Question 8

M1   *Moi, j'adore mon téléphone portable, je l'ai sur moi presque tout le temps. Malheureusement, les portables sont interdits au collège et **je dois le laisser chez moi**. Le soir j'envoie alors tous mes textos et **je bavarde avec des amis**.*

F1   *Les portables, **ça m'est égal**. Il y a certains qui pensent qu'ils sont utiles mais vraiment, les jeunes passent trop de temps dessus. C'est ennuyeux quand on va au resto et on est tous en train de texter ou de **se montrer des vidéos** au lieu de se parler.*

F2   *J'aime bien quand il l'a sur lui car **je m'inquiète un peu moins**. Quand il n'en avait pas il oubliait toujours de me dire où il était. En plus **il m'explique comment utiliser toutes les applications**.*

Mark Scheme:

0-6	- Award one mark for each correct answer, up to six. - Incorrect answers score 0 marks for that question.

L'environnement

9 Que dit Aurélie?	
A	[1]
C	[1]
D	[1]
F	[1]
K	[1]
L	[1]

TOP TIP: Use your time wisely.

Remember that you have five minutes before the start of all the recordings to look at the questions. Use this time to <u>underline the key words</u> in each sentence. Make notes, or try to write out the key words in English.

When you listen to the recording, your underlined words will help you focus on the key information.

For this type of question, you need to listen carefully to the information you hear in the recording and compare it to the sentences in the table. **Make sure that you have read them first!** There are **six** marks, one for each cross in a correct box. Check that you have exactly six answers crossed when you reach the end of the question.

The answers occur in order in the recording, which will help you to keep track. Listen out for **common phrases** and **synonyms** for words used in the sentences.

Full transcript for Question 9

M1   *Aurélie, d'où venez-vous?*

F1   *Je viens de l'île Maurice, qui se trouve dans l'ouest de l'océan Indien.*

M1   *Et ça fait combien de temps que vous êtes ici en France?*

F1   ***Mes parents ont déménagés*** *ici* ***quand j'avais dix ans*** *pour le travail de mon père donc je suis ici depuis huit ans.*

M1   *Est-ce qu'il y avait des problèmes environnementaux chez vous en île Maurice?*

F1   ***Oui****, comme partout dans le monde. Nous avions beaucoup de pollution de l'eau et de l'air et en plus, il y a plusieurs espèces en voie d'extinction.*

M1   *Qu'est-ce que vous avez fait pour réduire cette pollution?*

F1   *Nous sommes toujours allés à l'école à pied et* ***nous avons systématiquement fait le recyclage.***

M1   *Et ici en France, qu'est-ce que vous faites pour l'environnement?*

F1 *Je ne prends jamais la voiture car je pense qu'il y en a trop dans les grandes villes, donc* **je me sers des transports en commun. Je n'utilise pas les sacs plastiques** *dans les supermarchés et j'apporte les miens.*

Mark Scheme:

0-6	- Award one mark for each correct answer, up to six. - If more than one box per question is crossed, then no marks are awarded.

Bien manger

---

10 Écoutez l'interview et notez les détails.

Manger sainement
Avantages:
Moins de problèmes avec nos dents [1]
Nous sentirons mieux [1]
Inconvénients:
(either of the two below) [1]
Ça prend du temps de cuisiner
C'est plus cher

Le petit déjeuner
Avantages:
(any two of the three below) [2]
Il nous donne de l'énergie
On est plus efficace
Ça aide à la concentration
Inconvénients:
Difficile de trouver des options saines [1]
Pas beaucoup de temps le matin [1]

For questions like this, it is essential to **jot down notes quickly in the margins as you go**, so that you can fill in the answers after hearing the second recording. The information isn't always in order, hence why noting down words can be helpful. Writing down **everything** you hear would be next to impossible and a waste of time, because not all of it is relevant to answering the question. You only need to write **short notes**.

Full sentences in listening papers aren't necessary (unless otherwise stated in the instructions) as there often isn't time.

TOP TIP: Write out words you don't know.

Get used to working out unfamiliar words when you hear them. **Write them down as accurately as you can** on a spare bit of the page, and see if they look similar to another word, either in French or in English: they may share a common root. For example, the word *frais* in the phrase *les produits frais* does look and sound similar to 'fresh'. If you don't know the word, then write it out phonetically: you can still pick up marks even if some words are misspelled (official mark schemes have guidelines for how close to the original spelling your answer must be).

Longer passages like this are designed to help the strongest candidates achieve top grades, and may contain unfamiliar words or terms. If you don't understand something that you hear, try to work it out from the context.

Full Transcript for Question 10

M1   *Bonjour Fabienne! Vous êtes chef d'un très bon restaurant.*

F1   *Oui, j'ai de la chance car je peux créer des plats sains. Si on mangeait plus sainement,* ***nous aurions moins de problèmes avec nos dents*** *car il y a beaucoup de boissons sucrées dans les magasins, et peut être la chose la plus importante, c'est que* ***nous nous sentons mieux*** *si on mange sainement. D'un autre côté, ça* ***prend du temps de cuisiner avec les produits frais*** *et* ***ils sont beaucoup plus chers.***

M1   *Agathe, qu'est-ce que vous pensez du petit déjeuner?*

F2   *Il ne faut jamais le rater car c'est le repas le plus important.* ***Il nous donne de l'énergie pour être efficace*** *tout au long de la journée et manger le matin nous* ***aide avec la concentration.*** *Si je me lève très tôt, c'est* ***difficile de trouver des options saines dans les magasins*** *et en plus, je n'ai* ***pas toujours beaucoup de temps le matin.***

Mark Scheme:

0-7	- Award one mark for each correct answer, up to seven. - Incorrect answers score 0 marks for that question. - For the advantages in 10(i), reject simply *moins de problèmes*: candidate should state that there are fewer problems with <u>teeth</u>. - Grammatical errors and spelling mistakes are accepted, as long as the answer is intelligible.

END OF SOLUTIONS FOR PAPER 1

Listening Paper 2

*Visit **www.rsleducational.co.uk/frenchaudio** to download the audio file for this paper.*

If you wish to complete this paper in timed conditions, allow 40 minutes plus 5 minutes' reading time.

Instructions

- Use **black** ink or ballpoint pen.
- Answer **all** questions.
- Answer the questions in the spaces provided.
  - *There may be more space than you require.*
- Dictionaries are **not** allowed.

Advice

- You have 5 minutes to read through the paper before the recording starts.
- You will hear each extract twice. You may write at any time during the examination. There will be a pause after each question.
- Read each question **carefully** before attempting it.
- The marks available for each question are given in [square brackets]. These give you an indication of how long to spend on it.
- There is a total of **50 marks** available for this paper.
- Leave time to check your answers at the end, if possible.

Answer ALL questions.

Le cinéma

1 Antoine parle d'un film qu'il a vu. Complétez les phrases en choisissant un mot dans la case.

Antoine is speaking about a film he saw. Complete the sentences by choosing a word from the box.

action   long   stupéfiants   nouveau
propre   aventure   importants
loin   décevants   près   court

Exemple: Il aime les films d'**action.**

(i) Le cinéma est ....

(ii) À son avis, le film était ....

(iii) Les effets spéciaux étaient ....

(iv) Il y avait peu de femmes avec des rôles ....

(v) Le cinéma est .... de sa maison.

(Total for Question 1 = 5 marks)

Mon école

2   Clément parle de son école. Comment est-elle ? Choisissez entre: **moderne(s),** **stricte(s), calme(s)** et **sympa(s)**. Chacun des mots peut être utilisé plusieurs fois.

Clément is speaking about his school. What's it like? Choose between: *moderne(s), stricte(s), calme(s)* and *sympa(s)*. Each word can be used more than once.

Exemple: Les élèves sont <u>sympas</u>

(i)   Son école est ....

(ii)   Les professeurs sont ....

(iii)   Son attitude est ....

(iv)   L'uniforme scolaire est ....

(v)   Le règlement est ....

(Total for Question 2 = 5 marks)

Faire du bénévolat

3   Écoutez cet entretien avec Céline.
Listen to an interview with Céline.

Écoutez et complétez les phrases en cochant [X] la bonne case pour chaque question.

Listen and complete the sentences by putting a cross [X] in the correct box for each question.

Exemple: How long has she volunteered for?

X	A 7 years.
	B 6 years.
	C Since she was 7 years old.
	D 6 months.

(i)   What is her job?

	A To prepare the food.
	B To wash the vegetables.
	C To cut the vegetables.
	D To clean the kitchen.

(ii)   Who comes to the soup kitchen?

	A Local people.
	B People in need.
	C Homeless people.
	D Elderly people.

(iii)   How does she feel about her work?

	A She is sad.
	B She is bored.
	C She has changed.
	D She enjoys it.

(Total for Question 3 = 3 marks)

Ma routine

4   Votre ami Frédéric parle de sa routine pendant les vacances.
    Your friend Frédéric is speaking about his routine during the holidays.

    De quoi parle-t-il? Écoutez et cochez [X] les **trois** bonnes cases.
    What does he talk about? Listen and put a cross [X] in the **three** correct boxes.

Exemple	why he likes holidays	X
A	where they went on holiday	
B	who he went on holiday with	
C	what he had for breakfast	
D	where they had lunch	
E	how many hours skiing in the afternoon	
F	his ski instructor	
G	where he will go skiing next year	

(Total for Question 4 = 3 marks)

Sous la Mer

5   Écoutez cette publicité à la radio
         Listen to this advert on the radio.

         Écoutez et complétez les phrases en cochant **[X]** la bonne case pour chaque
         question.

         Listen and complete the sentences by putting a cross **[X]** in the correct box for
         each question.

Exemple: Sous la mer is…

X	**A** an aqua park.
	B a theme park.
	C a park.
	D a beach.

(i)   Last year they received…

	A 2000 visitors.
	B 2 million visitors.
	C 20 000 visitors.
	D 40 000 visitors.

(ii)   It is open from mid-April until…

	A 20th October.
	B 25th September.
	C end of September.
	D 15th October.

(iii)   Last entrance is at…

	A 4:30pm.
	B 5:00pm.
	C 6:30pm.
	D 7:00pm.

(iv)   You can stay nearby in a…

A	hotel.
B	a campsite.
C	a hostel.
D	a bed and breakfast.

(v)   The tourist office can supply information on…

A	parking.
B	where to stay.
C	the town.
D	the beaches.

(Total for Question 5 = 4 marks)

La pauvreté en France

6　Écoutez ce reportage sur la pauvreté en France à la radio. Répondez aux questions suivantes en **anglais.**

Listen to this report on poverty in France on the radio. Respond to the following questions in **English.**

(i)　What is happening to the number of people living in poverty?　　　[1]

....

(ii)　According to the report, what is the most shocking fact about poverty in France?　　　[1]

....

(iii)　What has made the situation worse?　　　[1]

....

(iv)　What situation do we find ourselves in now? Give **one** example.　　　[2]

....

....

(Total for Question 6 = 4 marks)

Entretien avec Tsi, artiste de graffiti

7   Écoutez cet entretien avec Tsi, artiste renommé de graffiti. Répondez **en anglais**.

Listen to an interview with Tsi, a renowned graffiti artist. Answer **in English**.

(i)   Where did his interest in graffiti art come from? Give **one** example.   [1]

....

(ii)   What did he first start drawing on? Give **one** example.   [1]

....

(iii)   What was his inspiration? Give **one** example.   [1]

....

(iv)   What about his art is important for him?   [1]

....

(v)   Where does he paint now? Give **one** example.   [1]

....

(Total for Question 7 = 5 marks)

Les stages et les carrières

8   Écoutez cette discussion entre amis sur les stages et carrières. Cochez [X] la bonne case pour chaque question.

Listen to this discussion about work experience and careers among some friends. Put a cross [X] in the correct box for each question.

Exemple: Leila wants to…

	A	work for her father.
	B	study at university.
X	C	be a pharmacist.
	D	be a doctor.

(i)   At school, Leila…

	A	enjoys science.
	B	is good at science.
	C	finds science hard.
	D	spends a lot of time on science homework.

(ii)   Adrien worked…

	A	for his aunt.
	B	on a campaign.
	C	on a farm.
	D	for his father.

(iii)   He doesn't want to do this job because…

	A	he can't do the work.
	B	he doesn't like getting up.
	C	he would have to get up early.
	D	he is lazy.

(vi)   André found his work experience…

	A	tiring.
	B	hard, as he was unhappy.
	C	exciting.
	D	boring.

(v) Mathilde stayed…

	A in a hotel.
	B alone in an apartment.
	C with the other interns.
	D in a hostel.

(vi) Mathilde would change…

	A the computers.
	B her knowledge of computers.
	C the level of competition for the job.
	D her knowledge of the job specifications.

(Total for Question 8 = 6 marks)

Les fêtes en France

9   Écoutez ce reportage à la télé des fêtes en France. Répondez aux questions suivantes **en anglais**.

Listen to this report on TV about festivals in France. Answer the following questions **in English**.

Part (a)

(i)   What do we learn from the report about how Mardi Gras is celebrated? Give **one** detail.   [1]

....

(ii)   Where else in the world is Mardi Gras celebrated? Give **one** detail.   [1]

....

(iii)   Why is Nice famous for its Carnival? Give **two** details.   [2]

....

(iv)   What changes every year for the Carnival in Nice? Give **one** detail.   [1]

....

(v)   Other than chariots and marionettes, what else is present during the Nice Carnival?   [1]

....

Part (b)

(i)   Give one reason why the Carnival is popular.   [1]

....

(ii)   What else can you see during the Carnival? Give **one** detail.   [1]

....

(iii) Give two reasons why people might not like visiting Nice at this time of year.

[2]

....

....

(Total for Question 9 = 10 marks)

Les voitures électriques

10   Écoutez Héloïse parler des voitures électriques. Cochez **[X]** les **deux** bonnes cases pour chaque question.

Listen to Héloïse talking about electric cars. Put a cross **[X]** in the **two** correct boxes for each question.

(i)   What does Héloïse say about electric cars in 2017?

Exemple	There has been rise in the sale of electric cars.	X
A	Public opinion about the cars has stayed the same.	
B	Sales of hybrid cars have slowed down.	
C	It was the record year for sales.	
D	France is second in Europe for electric car sales.	
E	France wants to ban petrol and diesel cars.	

(ii)   What does Héloïse say about the advantages of electric cars?

Exemple	They are efficient.	X
A	They have zero emissions.	
B	They only make a small amount of noise.	
C	They are cheap to run.	
D	You don't have to charge the car too often.	
E	They can be quick cars to drive.	

(Total for Question 10 = 4 marks)

TOTAL FOR PAPER = 50 MARKS

Blank Page

Listening Paper 2 – SOLUTIONS

Le cinéma

1 Antoine parle d'un film qu'il a vu.	
Exemple *action*	
(i) *nouveau*	[1]
(ii) *long*	[1]
(iii) *stupéfiants*	[1]
(iv) *importants*	[1]
(v) *près*	[1]

This 'warm-up' question tests some fairly simple core GCSE vocabulary to do with films.

The key to answering these questions is to know plenty of synonyms and not always to expect the exact words provided in the box. In the first question, the speaker says that the cinema has just opened (*vient d'ouvrir*): the cinema is new and therefore you can write that it is *nouveau*. Question **(ii)** gives us the exact word needed for the answer in the recording, that the film was *long*. However, for question **(iii)**, you will need to know that *stupéfiants* means 'amazing' and is a synonym of *impressionnants*.

TOP TIP: Use grammar.

Look for **grammatical agreements** between the questions and the options in the answer box. Most of the options given are adjectives, with a few prepositions (*loin* and *près*). If the question is looking for a plural adjective then it will narrow things down. For example, in question **(iii)** it says *les effets spéciaux étaient...* and we know that 'special effects' is plural, so we have three options in the answers: *stupéfiants*, *importants* or *décevants*.

Full transcript for Question 1

M1 *Hier soir j'ai vu le **nouveau** film d'Idris Elba, parce que j'adore les films d'action. Le cinéma **vient d'ouvrir** dans ma ville. C'est un **long** film mais il ne m'a pas semblé long du tout, je voulais en voir plus. Il y avait plusieurs scènes de combats violents et les effets spéciaux étaient **impressionnants**. À mon avis, il n'y avait pas assez de femmes dans **les rôles principaux**. Ce qui est génial, c'est que le cinéma n'est qu'à **vingt minutes de** chez moi.*

Mark Scheme:

0-5	- Award one mark for each correct answer, up to five.

Mon école

2 Clément parle de son école	
Exemple *sympas*	
(i) *moderne*	[1]
(ii) *strictes*	[1]
(iii) *calme*	[1]
(iv) *moderne*	[1]
(v) *stricte*	[1]

This section is once again testing core vocabulary, as well as your ability to listen carefully and pinpoint important information.

The key skill required here is **inference**. We can infer that her school is modern because she says *notre école est nouveau*. Likewise, their school uniform is *à la mode*, so we can understand that this would fit with 'modern' as an answer.

There are no pauses here. It might help if you jot down the first few letters of the word that you think corresponds to the answer. You can do this in the space by the question numbers when you first listen to the recording. If you write out the whole word then you might miss the next piece of necessary information.

Full transcript for Question 2

M1 *Il y a 1000 élèves donc c'est assez grand mais tout le monde est très **sympa**. Mon école se trouve tout près d'Avignon. La ville est très vieille mais le bâtiment de **notre école est nouveau**. Je trouve qu'il y a **beaucoup de pression** de nos profs et **ils nous donnent trop de devoirs**. Mais moi, **je ne me stresse pas, je suis tranquille** car je suis assez travailleur. Tous les élèves peuvent porter un pantalon et l'uniforme est **à la mode**. Le règlement, par contre, est **très contrôlé** et **on ne peut jamais être en retard**.*

Mark Scheme:

0-5	- Award one mark for each correct answer, up to five. - Grammatical errors (e.g. with pluralisation) can be ignored.

Faire du bénévolat

> **3 Écoutez cet entretien avec Céline**
> **Exemple** *A*
> **(i)** *C*   [1]
> **(ii)** *C*   [1]
> **(iii)** *D*   [1]

It's important to remember that you don't always need to understand every word if you get the gist of a phrase. You are unlikely to have come across *la soupe populaire* or *une chaîne humaine* but you can guess the context: the recording mentions volunteer work and includes basic words for food.

Some questions rely on key vocabulary rather than inference. In **(ii)** you do need to know that the word *sans abri* means homeless.

Full transcript for Question 3

F1   *Ça fait sept ans que j'offre de l'aide bénévole dans ma ville. J'aide à la soupe populaire avec mes parents chaque fin de semaine. Nous formons une chaîne humaine pour cuisiner une grande quantité de nourriture et c'est à moi de **couper tous les légumes**. Il y a environ trente personnes qui sont **sans abri** qui viennent chaque fois et cela m'a permis de les connaître en parlant avec tout le monde. Je trouve que l'ambiance est positive et **ça me plait énormément**, je ne m'ennuie jamais.*

Mark Scheme:

0-3	- Award one mark for each correct answer, up to three. - If more than one box per question is crossed, then no marks are awarded.

Ma routine

> **4 Votre ami Frédéric parle de sa routine pendant les vacances**
> **(i)** *A*   [1]
> **(ii)** *D*   [1]
> **(iii)** *F*   [1]

With questions like these, try to mark the answers you don't think are correct with a small cross as you hear them. The information given in the recording mentions the word for breakfast (*petit déjeuner*) but it doesn't state *what* he ate for breakfast, and therefore **C** can be eliminated. We are told: *Je me levais chaque jour à huit heures pour* *manger un très bon petit déjeuner ... on mangeait le déjeuner sur les pistes de ski. Il y a un steak haché sublime!* We know that he ate a good breakfast and are then told what he likes to eat for lunch. The key information is that he had lunch in the mountains and so **D** can be selected.

Finally, in the last sentence, he states that he doesn't know if they will return next year, but he hopes so: **G** cannot be chosen, because of his uncertainty.

TOP TIP: Make good use of the five minutes before the exam starts.

Because **the speed picks up** through these exercises, it is very important that you spend time reading the questions in the five minutes given to you at the start of the paper. That will allow you to follow the recordings more easily and look out for the key information.

Full transcript for Question 4

M1 *J'adore les vacances car je peux me détendre. L'année dernière **nous sommes allés en Suisse** pour faire du ski. Je me levais chaque jour à huit heures pour manger un très bon petit déjeuner. Il fallait beaucoup manger car on faisait quatre heures de ski le matin. **On mangeait le déjeuner sur les pistes de ski.** Il y avait un steak haché sublime! Puis, l'après-midi, **j'allais avec mon moniteur** pour améliorer mes sauts à ski. Il était très sympa et je peux mieux sauter maintenant. Je ne sais pas si nous allons revenir l'année prochaine mais je l'espère.*

Mark Scheme:

0-3	- Award one mark for each correct answer, up to three. - If more than one box per question is crossed, then no marks are awarded.

Sous la Mer

5 Écoutez cette publicité à la radio.	
Exemple *A*	
(i) *C*	[1]
(ii) *B*	[1]
(iii) *B*	[1]
(iv) *D*	[1]
(v) *B*	[1]

This question is testing your **numbers, dates and times**. It's particularly important to revise these thoroughly, as they will almost certainly come up. The answers occur in the recording in order.

For question **(iv)**, you may not recognise the phrase *des chambres d'hôtes* as 'bed and breakfast', but if you try to translate the question into French, then by a process of elimination you can guess the answer. **A** would be *un hôtel*, **B** is *un camping* and **C** is *un auberge de jeunesse*.

Full transcript for Question 5

F1   *Bienvenue à Sous la Mer, le meilleur **parc d'attraction aquatique** en Provence-Alpes-Côte d'Azur. Chaque année nous recevons environ **vingt mille visiteurs** et nous sommes ouverts de mi-avril jusqu'au **vingt-cinq septembre**. On ouvre les robinets à huit heures trente le matin et **notre dernière entrée est à 17h**. Vous pouvez louer des cabines dans les arbres ou il y a **des chambres d'hôtes** à côté pour améliorer votre expérience. Le syndicat d'initiative est à dix minutes à pied et il peut vous fournir toutes **les informations de logement**.*

Mark Scheme:

0-4	- Award one mark for each correct answer, up to four. - If more than one box per question is crossed, then no marks are awarded.

La pauvreté en France

6 Écoutez ce reportage sur la pauvreté en France à la radio.	
(i) *it is going up*	[1]
(ii) *the number of children living in poverty*	[1]
(iii) *the economic crisis*	[1]
(iv) *the price of food increased* **or** *we have less money* **or** *products are more expensive*	[1]

This question asks you to write in English and you only need to write **short notes**. Full sentences in listening papers aren't necessary (unless otherwise stated in the instructions) as there often isn't time. You will have to be precise and accurate in your translation of the recording. In **(ii)**, writing 'children' isn't enough as what is shocking is the number of children who live in poverty.

The vocabulary used in the recordings is becoming more complicated as the exam progresses, so **aim to write as simply as possible** in English. The exercise requires you to be alert, in order to pick out specific bits of information from an interview. This tests both your core vocabulary and your general comprehension skills.

As seen in the **Top Tip: Write out the words you don't know** (**Paper 1**, solutions), if you don't recognise a word, write it down as accurately as you can on a spare bit of the page and then come back to it at the end of the question to see if you can work out what it means.

Question **(iv)** is looking for two pieces of information, so try to **make quick notes** during the first recording or you may run out of time. You don't need to write identical answers to those given above. As long as what you have put is **very close in meaning** – especially for the last question – then you will pick up marks.

There are many words in this piece which **sound like their English translations** and they can guide you through the recording. Listen out for *personnes, pauvreté, nombre, crise économique* and *revenue* which translate as 'people', 'poverty', 'number', 'economic crisis' and 'revenue'. You may notice that **superlatives** and **comparatives** are being tested here. You'll hear *le plus choquant* (the most shocking), *une situation…est devenue encore pire* (the situation has got worse), *nous avons moins d'argent* (we have less money) and *les produits sont plus chers* (products are more expensive).

Full transcript for Question 6

M1   *Selon un sondage récent, il y a actuellement presque quinze pourcent de personnes en France qui vivent sous le seuil de pauvreté et **ce taux de pauvreté augmente chaque année**. Le plus choquant, c'est **le nombre d'enfants** qui vivent dans des conditions inhumaines.*

M1   *Salma travaille dans ce secteur, écoutons son témoignage.*

F1   *Nous nous trouvons dans une situation désastreuse et elle est devenue encore pire **depuis la crise économique** qui a affecté plusieurs pays. Le revenu de beaucoup de ménages est considérablement réduit et beaucoup de parents ont perdu leurs emplois, en outre **le prix de la nourriture a augmenté**. Par conséquent, **nous avons moins d'argent** et **les produits sont plus chers**.*

Mark Scheme:

0-4	- Award one mark for each correct answer, up to four.

Entretien avec Tsi, artiste de graffiti

7 Écoutez cet entretien avec Tsi	
(i) *his cousin* **or**	
he was shown places with graffiti on them	[1]
(ii) *notepad* **or**	
any piece of paper **or**	
t-shirts	[1]
(iii) *other young artists* **or** *the countries he visited/travelled to*	[1]
(iv) *to have an impact on people/to affect people*	[1]
(v) *abandoned places* **or** *abandoned buildings*	[1]

The technique for this question is very similar to **Question 6**. The only difference is that it is slightly harder. Apply your knowledge of vocabulary and your comprehension skills to extract the relevant information from the recording. Be wary of writing too much as only short phrases are needed.

For **(i)**, the speaker immediately tells us that he discovered graffiti through his cousin and that he was shown places with graffiti on them. Either point is fine. You will sometimes find that several different pieces of information could be used to answer a question, so go with the one you are sure of and that you understand best.

Full transcript for Question 7

F1 *Comment est-ce que vous avez découvert le graffiti?*

M1 *C'était **grâce à mon cousin** à l'âge de treize ans. Il m'a montré **des endroits avec des graffiti** car ça l'intéressait. J'ai aimé le design et donc j'ai commencé à **faire des dessins dans mon bloc-notes** ou **n'importe quel papier**. Nous avons commencé à **créer des t-shirts** avec des slogans.*

F1 *Après le collège où est-ce que vous êtes allés?*

M1 *J'ai fini mes études et puis j'ai décidé de voyager, d'être indépendant et je suis allé jusqu'en Australie. C'est là-bas que j'ai rencontré plein **d'autres jeunes artistes. Ils m'ont beaucoup influencé** et **chaque pays que j'ai visité aussi**. J'ai commencé à comprendre le message que je voulais créer à travers mon art.*

F1 *Quel est ce message?*

M1 *Pour moi c'était très important d'**avoir un impact sur les gens**, et j'ai décidé de me concentrer sur « les oubliés ». Cela fait référence aux **endroits et aux bâtiments abandonnés** et les gens aussi.*

Mark Scheme:

0-5	- Award one mark for each correct answer, up to five. - No mark if answer indicates guesswork.

Les stages et les carrières

8 Écoutez cette discussion sur les stages et carrières.	
Exemple *C*	
(i) *B*	[1]
(ii) *C*	[1]
(iii) *C*	[1]
(iv) *D*	[1]
(v) *C*	[1]
(vi) *B*	[1]

It's especially important here to **listen out for key vocabulary** and **avoid being swayed by common traps**.

In the example we hear the word for father (*père*), which may make you think she wants to work for her father **(A)**. The other trap is that she mentions *médicine* when she says that all her family work in medicine: you might think of answer **D**, that she wants to be a doctor. In fact, she says that she wants to be a pharmacist, *je voudrais être pharmacienne*, which leads us to answer **C**.

Adrien says (question **(ii)**) that he worked for some friends of his father, near his aunt, which might trick you into looking at answers **A** and **D**. The word *campagne* sounds similar to 'campaign', but the key word you're looking out for is *ferme*: farm. If you didn't get that word, then you might notice that he doesn't want to be a farmer, *je ne veux pas être fermier*, and also that he doesn't like animals, *je n'aime pas trop les animaux*.

In **(iii)** he says that one would have to get up early each morning and he couldn't do that every day. When you hear *je ne pouvais pas faire ça*, this may lead you to thinking that he *couldn't* do the work, so that you choose **A** – but it is referring to getting up early. We also hear the word *parasseux*, but it is expressed in a **negative sentence**, confirming that he is **not** lazy: therefore, the answer cannot be **D**. He never states that he doesn't like getting up, but he does say that he would have to get up **early**: the answer is **C**.

André **(iv)** is very positive about being a lawyer at the start (potential for answer **C**), but then mentions that his co-workers were unhappy, *mécontents*, which might lead you to tick **B**. However, he then states that he was bored, *ennuyeux*, so we know that the answer is **D**.

Mathilde states that she had to share a flat with other interns, so knowledge of the verb 'to share', *partager* and the noun 'interns', *stagiaires* would help in the sentence: *partager un appartement avec les autres stagiaires*. The final question is looking for an understanding of *d'avoir une meilleure connaissance* as she says that she needs a better knowledge of computers.

Full transcript for Question 8

F1   *Leila, qu'est-ce que vous voulez faire plus tard dans la vie?*

F2   *Moi, je veux être comme mon père, je voudrais être pharmacienne. Toute ma famille travaille dans la médecine et donc j'ai de la chance, car au collège **je trouve les sciences très faciles**.*

F1   *Et vous, Adrien?*

M1   *Mes parents m'ont demandé de faire un stage donc j'ai travaillé pour des amis de mon père qui ont **une ferme** à la campagne près de chez ma tante. Je sais très bien que je ne veux pas être fermier, je n'aime pas trop les animaux et **il faut se lever trop tôt chaque matin mais je ne pourrais pas faire ça tous les jours** et ne je suis pas paresseux.*

F1   *André, est-ce que vous avez fait un stage?*

M1   *J'ai toujours voulu être avocat donc j'ai fait un stage dans un cabinet mais je ne veux plus faire ce métier. C'était vraiment **ennuyeux** et tous les employés avaient l'air d'être très mécontents.*

F1   *Et vous Mathilde?*

F2   *Je suis partie en Espagne pendant trois mois cet été et c'était très intéressant. **J'ai dû partager un appartement avec les autres stagiaires** et j'étais très nerveuse mais tout le monde était sympa. La seule chose que je changerais est **d'avoir une meilleure connaissance en informatique** avant d'y aller car c'est essentiel d'avoir ces compétences.*

Mark Scheme:

0-6	- Award one mark for each correct answer, up to six. - If more than one box per question is crossed, then no marks are awarded.

Les fêtes en France

---

9 Écoutez ce reportage à la télé.

Part (a)

(i) *parades* **or**
   dancing in the street **or**
   delicious food [1]

(ii) *Guadeloupe* **or**
   Martinique [1]

(iii) *oldest festival* **and**
   welcomes more than a million visiers [2]

(iv) *a different theme each year* [1]

(v) *flowers* [1]

Part (b)

 (i) *it's ideal for families* **or**
   kids are the most important **or**
   it's a real experience for all the senses [1]

(ii) *dancers* **or**
   musicians [1]

(iii) (any two of the below)
   the hotels are busy **or**
   hard to find a place to stay in the centre **or**
   there are crowds **or**
   there are a lot of people [2]

This recording gives a lot of information at once, so note down your answers quickly. Much of the information required relates to your knowledge of key vocabulary, such as the answers to questions **(i)**, **(ii)** and **(iv)** in **Part (a)**. You need to understand *parades*, *danses dans la rue* and *nourriture délicieuse*. Question **(iii)** is asking for two pieces of information: make sure to check how many marks are required for each question and if additional material is needed.

Part (b) of the question goes into further detail and gives you more options. Look out for key words to help you find your place in the recording, such as *le carnival est populaire car…* meaning that 'the carnival is popular because', which leads into the answer for question **(i)**. There's another clue when she says *le seul inconvénient*, meaning 'the only inconvenience', which alerts us to the information needed for question **(iii)**.

Full transcript for Question 9

Part (a)

F1   *Mardi Gras est une fête pour célébrer le festin des mets gras avant la longue période de 40 jours, de carême. On le fête avec des **parades**, des **danses dans la rue** et, bien sûr, beaucoup de **nourriture délicieuse**. On le fête partout dans le monde y compris en **Guadeloupe** et en **Martinique** mais peut-être le Carnaval le plus célèbre et celui de Nice parce que c'est le plus **ancien** et la ville de Nice **accueille plus d'un million de visiteurs** chaque année en février ou mars. Chaque année il y a **un thème différent** et l'année dernière le thème était celui de la gastronomie. Les rues sont remplies de chars et de marionnettes. Aussi, on peut voir **les batailles de fleurs** qui sont magnifiques.*

[PAUSE]

Part (b)

F1   *Le carnaval est très populaire car **c'est idéal pour les familles**, et **les enfants sont certainement les plus importants**. Avec des **danseurs** et des **musiciens** excellents, c'est une **vraie expérience pour tous les sens** et pour tout le monde. À la fin de la fête il y a des feux d'artifices merveilleux, une tradition importante. Le seul inconvénient, c'est que **tous les hôtels sont occupés** et donc c'est difficile de trouver un logement au centre-ville. Et si vous n'aimez pas **la foule**, faites attention car **il y aura beaucoup de monde**!*

Mark Scheme:

0-10	- Award one mark for each correct answer, up to ten. - No mark if evidence of guesswork.

Les voitures électriques

10 Écoutez Héloïse parler des voitures électriques.	
(i) C, E	[2]
(ii) A, D	[2]

This final question is an opportunity to score four marks by isolating four specific, separate points from a fairly long passage of dialogue.

The first answer cannot be **A**, as the recording states that the French have started to change their opinion (*les français ont bien commencé à changer leur opinion*). **B** isn't an option as there has been a rise (*une progression*) in the market for hybrid models. Finally, **D** isn't an option as France is the first country in Europe (*le fort leader*).

For the second question, you can eliminate **B** because the cars are completely silent (*elles roulent complètement silencieusement*), as well as **C**, because the recording doesn't state that they are cheap to run but it does give another positive opinion: that in the long term there are financial benefits (*au long terme il y a des bienfaits*). Their speed is their downfall (*le seul inconvénient reste toujours être leur vitesse*), which allows you to discount **E**. In order to get **A**, you needed to understand that they don't contribute to air pollution and that their energy is clean. Finally, for **D**, it is necessary to understand that their batteries last for a long time (*des batteries qui durent longtemps*).

Full transcript for Question 10 (i) and (ii)

F1   *Cette année, nous avons vu une grande augmentation du taux de voitures électriques vendus en France, donc peut-être on peut dire que les français ont bien commencé à changer leur opinion envers ce type de véhicule. Nous voyons aussi une progression dans le marché des modèles hybrides. 2017 a été **la meilleure année de ventes de voitures électriques en France** et maintenant la France est le leader européen des véhicules électriques, même devant la Norvège. **La vision d'interdire les véhicules diesel et essence en France peut devenir une réalité.***

[PAUSE]

F1   *Evidemment, il y a plusieurs avantages aux voitures électriques. Premièrement leur efficacité est impressionnante, elles ne sont plus une idée de la science-fiction. Ensuite, ces voitures **ne contribuent pas à la pollution atmosphérique** car leur **énergie est propre** et elles roulent complètement silencieusement, ce qui est utile dans les villes bruyantes. Puis, financièrement, au long terme il y a des bienfaits et maintenant les nouveaux modèles ont **des batteries qui durent longtemps**. Le seul inconvénient reste toujours leur vitesse.*

Mark Scheme:

0-4	- Award one mark for each correct answer, up to four. - If more than two boxes per question are crossed, then no marks are awarded.

END OF SOLUTIONS FOR PAPER 2

Listening Paper 3

Visit **www.rsleducational.co.uk/frenchaudio** to download the audio file for this paper.

If you wish to complete this paper in timed conditions, allow 40 minutes plus 5 minutes' reading time.

Instructions

- Use **black** ink or ballpoint pen.
- Answer **all** questions.
- Answer the questions in the spaces provided.
    - *There may be more space than you require.*
- Dictionaries are **not** allowed.

Advice

- You have 5 minutes to read through the paper before the recording starts.
- You will hear each extract twice. You may write at any time during the examination. There will be a pause after each question.
- Read each question **carefully** before attempting it.
- The marks available for each question are given in [square brackets]. These give you an indication of how long to spend on it.
- There is a total of **50 marks** available for this paper.
- Leave time to check your answers at the end, if possible.

Answer ALL questions.

Une excursion en bateau

Cochez [X] la bonne case A, B, C ou D pour chaque question.
Put a cross [X] in the right box A, B, C or D for each question.

1   Vous êtes à Bruxelles.
       You are in Brussels.

(i)   Vous êtes à l'office de tourisme. Vous voulez faire une excursion en bateau.
       You're at the tourist office. You want to go on a boat trip.

De quel quai part le bateau?
What quay does the boat leave from?

A	B	C	D
quai 4	**quai 6**	**quai 8**	**quai 10**

(ii)   Vous demandez à quelle heure est le départ du bateau.
       You ask what time the boat leaves.

À quelle heure est le départ du bateau?
What time does the boat leave?

A	B	C	D
16h10	**17h50**	**13h20**	**16h30**

(iii)   Vous demandez ce que vous verrez pendant l'excursion.
             You ask what you will see during the trip.

Qu'est-ce qu'il y a à voir pendant le voyage?
What is there to see during the trip?

(iv)   Vous allez au restaurant. Qu'est-ce que vous commandez?
            You go to a restaurant. What do you order?

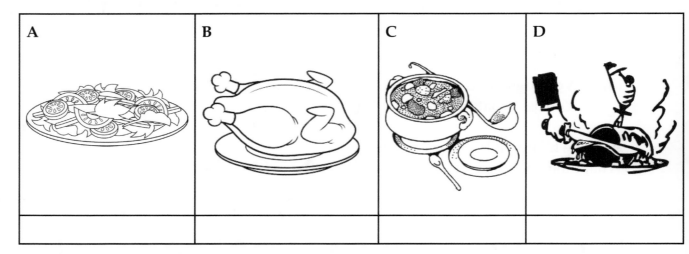

(v)   Vous demandez des directions.
     You ask for directions.

Où se trouve le supermarché?
Where is the supermarket?

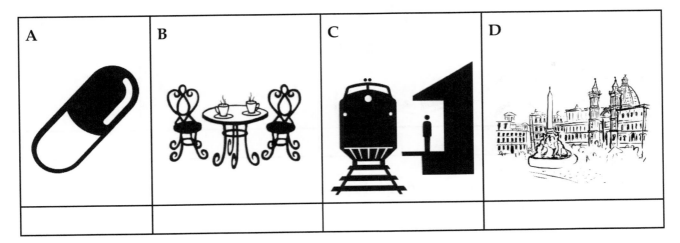

(vi)   Qu'est-ce que vous voulez faire demain?
      What do you want to do tomorrow?

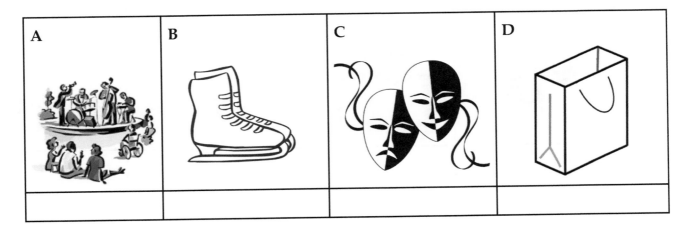

(vii) Vous avez laissé quelque chose à l'hôtel. Qu'est-ce que vous avez oublié?

You've left something at the hotel. What have you forgotten?

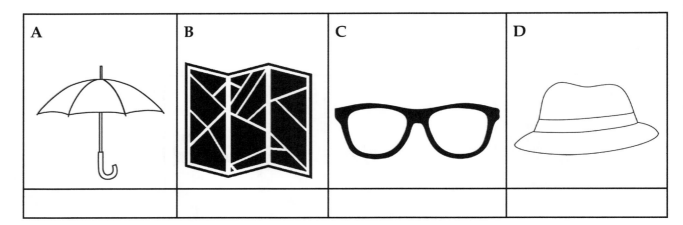

(viii) Votre ami vous demande quel était ton moment préféré. Qu'est-ce que vous lui répondez?

Your friend asks you want your favourite moment was. What you do you reply?

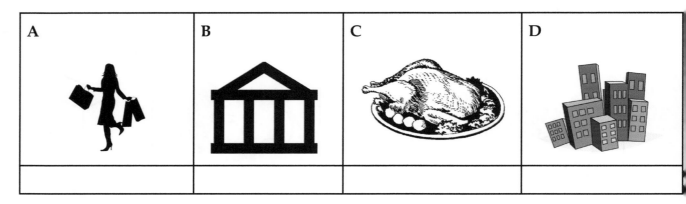

(Total for Question 1 = 8 marks)

Bordeaux à vélo

Répondez **en français** ou cochez **[X]** la bonne case pour chaque question.
Answer **in French** or put a cross **[X]** in the correct box for each question.

2   Vous allez entendre une annonce pour louer des vélos à Bordeaux.
You're going to listen to an advert about renting bicycles in Bordeaux.

(i)   Il est bien de visiter Bordeaux entre juin et ………………

(ii)   Qu'est-ce qu'on peut éviter…

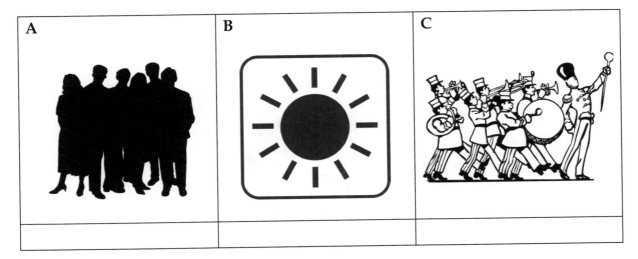

(iii)   La route commence devant…

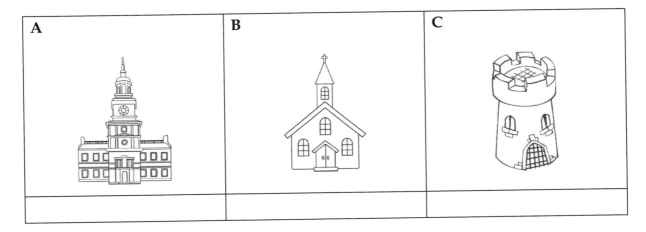

(iv)   Bordeaux est célèbre pour…

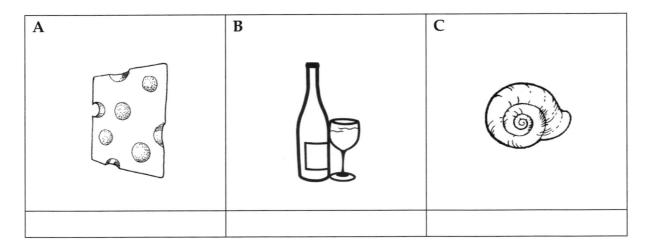

(v)   Il ne faut pas manquer…

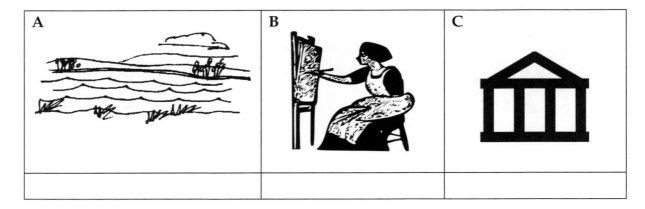

(vi)   Prix ……………… euros.

(vii)   Il faut payer pour…

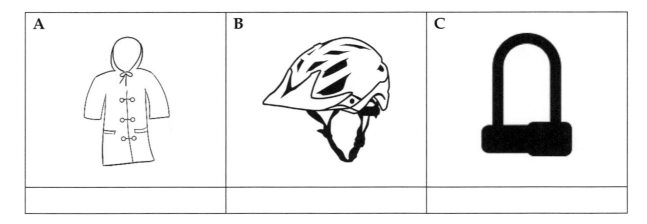

(Total for Question 2 = 7 marks)

La forme et la santé

Cochez [X] les cases si les affirmations sont **vraies**.
Put a cross [X] in the box if the statements are **true**.

3   Écoutez quatre jeunes qui parlent de la forme et de la santé.
     Listen to four young people speak about their bodies and their health.

Cochez seulement **6 cases**.
Only cross **6 boxes**.

(i)	Léo	Vrai
A	Léo aime le petit déjeuner.	
B	Léo préfère boire un café.	
C	Léo mange le petit déjeuner très tôt.	

(ii)	Lina	Vrai
D	Lina pense qu'il faut interdire les publicités sur le tabac.	
E	Lina veux être mieux informée sur les effets du tabac.	
F	Les parents de Lina pensent qu'elle fume.	

(iii)	Jules	Vrai
G	Jules ne s'intéresse pas à bien manger.	
H	Jules ne mange jamais de la nourriture malsaine.	
I	Jules ne mange pas de sucreries pendant la semaine.	

(iv)	Lucas	Vrai
J	Lucas ne fait plus beaucoup de sport.	
K	Lucas peut aller à la gym au collège.	
L	Lucas trouve qu'il se relaxe quand il fait du sport.	

(Total for Question 3 = 6 marks)

Le Nouveau-Brunswick

4   Vous allez entendre deux interviews avec Olivier et Béatrice. Ils viennent de Nouveau-Brunswick au Canada et ils parlent de leur région. **Questions (i) à (v)**: dans chaque phrase, il y a un détail qui ne correspond pas à l'extrait. Écrivez le(s) mot(s) juste(s) **en français**.

You're going to hear two interviews with Olivier and Béatrice. They come from New Brunswick in Canada and they are talking about their region. **Questions (i) to (v)**: in each sentence, there is a detail which doesn't match the extract. Write the correct word(s) **in French**.

Écoutez Olivier.

(i)   La ville se situe ~~dans le nord~~   .... [1]

(ii)   Il y a beaucoup de ~~montagnes~~   .... [1]

(iii)   Olivier aime bien ~~le temps~~   .... [1]

(iv)   Olivier va étudier ~~le tourisme~~   .... [1]

(v)   Quand il peut, Olivier fait ~~la cuisine~~   .... [1]

Écoutez Béatrice.

(vi)   Quand est-ce qu'elle est partie?   [1]

....

(vii)   Qu'est-ce qu'elle fait à Québec?   [1]

....

(viii)   Qu'est-ce qu'elle veut faire à l'avenir? Donnez **3** détails.   [3]

....

....

....

(ix) Selon Béatrice, pourquoi elle a pris sa décision? Donnez **2** détails. [2]

....

....

(Total for Question 4 = 12 marks)

La cuisine

Cochez [X] la bonne case A, B ou C pour chaque question.
Put a cross [X] in the correct box A, B or C for each question.

5   Vous allez entendre une interview avec Yousef, jeune chef algérien.
You're going to hear an interview with Yousef, a young Algerian cook.

(i)   Qu'est-ce que Yousef va faire maintenant?

A	Prendre une pause	
B	Rentrer au travail	
C	Aller en vacances	

(ii)   Qu'est-ce qu'il va faire en Inde?

A	Se relaxer	
B	Manger de la nourriture	
C	Cuisiner	

(iii)   Avec qui est-ce qu'il voyage?

A	Son patron	
B	Sa sœur	
C	Son ami	

(iv)   Pourquoi est-ce qu'il y va?

A	Pour ouvrir un restaurant	
B	Pour une compétition	
C	Pour voir le pays	

(v)   Qui l'a inspiré?

A	Son père	
B	Sa sœur	
C	Sa mère	

(vi)   Pourquoi aime-t-il cuisiner?

A	Pour passer du temps avec des amis	
B	Il l'a toujours fait	
C	Sa famille aime ses repas	

(Total for Question 5 = 6 marks)

L'argent de poche

Écoutez l'extrait et répondez aux questions suivantes **en français**.
Listen to the extract and answer the following questions **in French**.

6   Vous allez entendre une interview avec Florent qui parle de l'argent de poche qu'il reçoit.

You're going to hear an interview with Florent who is speaking about pocket money.

(i)   Qu'est-ce qu'il peut acheter avec son argent de poche?   [1]

....

(ii)   S'il veut acheter quelque chose qui coûte cher, qu'est-ce qu'il doit faire?
Donnez **deux** détails.   [2]

....

....

(iii)   Qu'est-ce qu'il a acheté quand il était plus jeune? Donnez **deux** détails.   [2]

....

....

(iv)   Que s'est-il passé quand il avait seize ans?   [1]

....

(v)   Qu'est-ce qu'il fait pour gagner de l'argent?   [1]

....

(vi)   Qu'est-ce qu'il a fait avec son salaire? Donnez **un** détail.   [1]

....

(vii) Selon lui, pourquoi c'est bien d'avoir un emploi? [1]

....

(viii) Qu'est-ce qu'il dit de son emploi? Donnez **deux** détails. [2]

....

....

(Total for Question 6 = 11 marks)

TOTAL FOR PAPER = 50 MARKS

Listening Paper 3 – SOLUTIONS

Une excursion en bateau

1 Vous êtes à Bruxelles	
(i) *C*	[1]
(ii) *A*	[1]
(iii) *C*	[1]
(iv) *C*	[1]
(v) *A*	[1]
(vi) *A*	[1]
(vii) *A*	[1]
(viii) *D*	[1]

The information in the question, as well as the title, gives you an idea as to what area of your core vocabulary is being tested: city and holidays. Times and numbers also come up, as is common in the first couple of questions in an exam.

Use the pause before the recording to **think of the principal words that might correspond to the pictures**, as well as **synonyms** that you might hear. For **(iii)**, you might think of *un café* (a café), *une cathédrale* (a cathedral), *un château* (a castle) and *une place* (a square). In this case, she mentions the castle.

Full transcript for Question 1

M1	*De quel quai part le bateau?*
F1	*Les excursions en bateau partent du quai **numéro 8**.*
M1	*À quelle heure part le bateau?*
F1	*Le bateau part à **seize heures dix**.*
M1	*Qu'est-ce qu'il y a à voir pendant le voyage?*
F1	*Il y a plein de choses à voir, comme notre célèbre **château**.*
M1	*Qu'est-ce que vous commandez?*
F1	*Pour moi, je voudrais **la soupe** du jour s'il vous plait.*
M1	*Où se trouve le supermarché?*
F1	*Le supermarché ? C'est à côté de **la pharmacie**.*
M1	*Qu'est-ce que vous voulez faire demain?*
F1	*Ben, j'ai envie **d'écouter de la musique**. Peut-on aller à un **concert**?*
M1	*Qu'est-ce que vous avez oublié?*
F1	*Ah non, il faut que je rentre à l'hôtel. J'ai oublié **mon parapluie**.*
M1	*Qu'est-ce que vous lui répondez?*
F1	*Pour moi, c'était l'architecture. J'ai adoré **les bâtiments**.*

Mark Scheme:

0-8	- Award one mark for each correct answer, up to eight. - If more than one box per question is crossed, then no marks are awarded.

Bordeaux à vélo

2 Vous entendez une annonce pour louer des vélos à Bordeaux	
(i) *août*	[1]
(ii) *A*	[1]
(iii) *B*	[1]
(iv) *B*	[1]
(v) *C*	[1]
(vi) *9.50*	[1]
(vii) *A*	[1]

This section tests your ability to listen carefully and pinpoint the key information, based on your knowledge of core vocabulary.

Once you have completed this section, **check your answers**. Make sure you have answered everything, and that you don't have multiple answers for a single question. If you have, erase or put a neat line through the wrong answer (**X**), to signal to the examiner that you have changed your mind.

TOP TIP: Dedicate time to learning vocab.
All the vocabulary tested here is in your GCSE syllabus. Try to **spend at least ten minutes a day learning vocab**: it will really help with the exam! There are plenty of free apps out there to help make it fun.

Full transcript for Question 2

F1   *Bordeaux est la troisième meilleure ville cyclable, après Amsterdam et Copenhague. La meilleure période pour partir dans notre ville merveilleuse est entre juin et **août**, mais si vous voulez **éviter la foule**, il faut venir au printemps ou en automne.*

*Faire votre tour de la ville à vélo. Notre route part de la Place Gambetta **devant l'église** et vous allez voir tous les monuments spectaculaires. Bordeaux est **bien connu pour le vin donc** faites attention de ne pas boire avant le tour. En fait, il y a même **un musée** dédié au vin – **il faut absolument le visiter**. Pour ceux âgés entre six et dix–sept ans l'entré est **neuf euros cinquante**.*

*Vous pouvez louer des vélos quelques heures ou à la une semaine mais le coût n'inclue pas **d'imperméables**!*

Mark Scheme:

0-7	- Award one mark for each correct answer, up to seven.
	- If more than one box per question is crossed, then no marks are awarded.

La forme et la santé

3 Écoutez quatre jeunes qui parlent de la forme et de la santé	
(i) *B*	[1]
(ii) *E, F*	[2]
(iii) *I*	[1]
(iv) *J, L*	[2]

Note here that **more than one box can be ticked per person**!

For **(i)**, Léo says that he knows it's necessary to eat a good breakfast, but he doesn't do that during the week as he gets up too early: *je me lève très tôt*, so the answer is **B**. Be careful not to cross **C**, with the mention of *le petit déjeuner* and *tôt*. There's a lot of dialogue given for just one answer so try to focus and listen to as much as you can. You don't want to miss vital clues, or information which will allow you to eliminate some options.

Lina, in **(ii)**, does not say that tobacco adverts should be stopped but that they should be reduced, *nous devons réduire la promotion*. She goes on to talk about education on the dangers of tobacco (the correct answer, **E**) and that she has explained to her parents that she doesn't smoke – but that they think she's lying. This is a more complicated way of saying that Lina's parents think she smokes (**F**). **Look out for information given indirectly like this**.

In **(iii)**, Jules says that he makes a huge effort to eat healthily (eliminating **G**), *je fais un grand effort pour manger bien et équilibré*, and that he tries to only eat snacks at the weekend, *j'essaye de manger des snacks que le weekend*, thus eliminating **H** and confirming **I** as the correct answer.

In **(iv)** you need to be on the lookout for **synonyms**. Jules says that he needs to relax and de-stress and sport helps him do this (*j'ai besoin de me détendre et le sport m'aide beaucoup*). The question uses the verb *se relaxer* and here we see the synonym: *se détendre*.

Full transcript for Question 3

M1   *Salut, je m'appelle Léo. Je sais bien qu'il faut manger un bon petit déjeuner mais je ne le fait pas pendant la semaine car je me lève très tôt. Pour moi, **le plus important, c'est de boire du café le matin**. Je n'aime pas trop le matin et je n'ai pas faim et vraiment, je n'ai pas beaucoup de temps. Je préfère prendre mon temps le weekend et manger avec mes amis vers onze heures. La nourriture à sept heures du matin, ça ne m'intéresse pas.*

F1   *Bonjour, je m'appelle Lina. On sait tous que le tabac est malsain mais c'est difficile car la majorité de mes amis fument. Je pense que nous devons réduire la promotion du tabac à travers les médias et **l'éducation sur les dangers du tabagisme doit être renforcée parmi les étudiants** ou sinon il faut avoir des lois plus strictes. **J'ai expliqué à mes parents que je ne fume pas mais ils pensent que je mens** car mes vêtements puent après avoir été avec mes amis.*

M1   *Salut, je m'appelle Jules. Je fais un grand effort pour manger bien et équilibré. Je mange plein de légumes et j'évite de manger des sucreries mais ce n'est pas facile car j'adore le chocolat, donc **j'essaye de manger des snacks que le weekend**. Il faut trouver un équilibre car ce n'est pas juste de se priver tout le temps.*

M1   *Bonjour, je m'appelle Lucas. L'année dernière j'ai fait de l'exercice trois fois par semaine mais **cette année j'ai plus de devoirs et donc je trouve difficile d'avoir assez de temps pour aller à la gym**, je ne sais pas quoi faire. Au collège on ne fait qu'une heure de sport par semaine et à mon avis, ce n'est pas suffisant. **J'ai besoin de me détendre et le sport m'aide beaucoup**.*

Mark Scheme:

0-6	- Award one mark for each correct answer, up to six.

Nouveau-Brunswick

4 Vous allez entendre deux interviews avec Olivier et Béatrice.	
(i) *le sud*	[1]
(ii) *forêts*	[1]
(iii) *les paysages*	[1]
(iv) *l'agriculture*	[1]
(v) *faire de l'équitation*	[1]
(vi) *à l'age de 18 ans*	[1]
(vii) *étudiante*	[1]
(viii) *prendre des vacances, aller en France, faire un stage **or** étudier aux États Unis*	[3]
(ix) *elle veut explorer, rencontrer des gens, voyager, étudier*	[2]

The first part of this question requires you to fill in the correct words to finish the sentences. You will often come across a recording set in another French-speaking country, perhaps in Africa, the Caribbean, the Pacific or Canada. **The change of location will not affect you in terms of vocabulary**.

This recording mentions two areas (the *sud-est* and the *sud*), but note that the question asks for the **town's** location, in which case *dans le sud* is the correct answer.

In part **(b)** we hear that Béatrice lived in the region all her life, for eighteen years (*j'ai habité ici toute ma vie, pendant dix-huit ans*), so we can therefore assume that she left at 18.

The last two questions begin to get more complicated as more information is required, without there being gaps in the recording. **Note down the information briefly** in the spaces around the question – then fill in the answers when you have time. She says she wants holidays (*je veux prendre des vacances*), to go to France to work (*aller en France pour travailler*) or to go to France to do an internship (*faire un stage*). To work and to do an internship would be accepted as two separate pieces of information. Finally, she says that she wants to do more studies in the USA (*faire encore des études aux États-Unis*). You have a lot of options here so it is important to be attentive and make as many notes as possible. Similarly for question **(ix)**, you have three options from which you should select two, for a two mark answer. I have highlighted all three options below.

Full transcript for Question 4

Part (a)

F1	Bon, Olivier, vous venez d'où exactement?
M1	Je suis né à Nouveau-Brunswick au Canada dans le sud-est du pays. J'habite à Saint-Jean, une grande ville **dans le sud** de la région.
F1	Décris-moi la région?
M1	C'est une province énorme avec plusieurs parcs nationaux et nous avons beaucoup de **forêts** sauvages.
F1	Qu'est-ce vous aimez le plus là-bas?
M1	Bon, ça ne va pas être la météo car nous avons des saisons impossibles – en hiver on a des grosses tempêtes de neige. Cependant, **les paysages** sont impressionnants.
F1	Est-ce que vous allez rester à Saint-Jean ?
M1	Oui, pour l'instant puis ensuite je veux aller à l'université à Montréal pour étudier **l'agriculture** car la faculté est très réputée.
F1	Qu'est-ce que vous faites de votre temps libre?
M1	Il y a plein de choses à faire en termes d'activités en plein air. Ce que j'adore faire le weekend, c'est de **faire de l'équitation** dans le parc national avec mes amis.

Part (b)

M1 *Alors Béatrice, vous venez de Nouveau-Brunswick aussi?*

F1 *Oui, j'ai habité ici toute ma vie, pendant **dix-huit ans** et puis j'ai déménagé à Québec où je suis **étudiante** en biotechnologie.*

M1 *Et après les études, qu'est-ce que vous voulez faire plus tard?*

F1 ***Je veux prendre des vacances** et après je voudrais **aller en France** pour **travailler** ou **faire un stage** car je veux travailler dans l'industrie pharmaceutique. J'ai de la chance car je viens d'une province bilingue, pas tout le monde parle français mais moi, je parle les deux, le français et l'anglais. Alors, peut-être je pourrais aller faire **encore des études aux États-Unis**. En fait, je vais y aller.*

M1 *Pourquoi est-ce que vous voulez partir?*

F1 *Je **veux explorer** et **rencontrer les gens** et pour moi, surtout pour quelqu'un qui étudie la biotechnologie, **c'est important de voyager et d'étudier**.*

Mark Scheme:

0-12	- Award one mark for each correct answer, up to twelve. - No mark for indicating guesswork.

La cuisine

5 Vous allez entendre une interview avec Yousef, jeune chef algérien.	
(i) *A*	[1]
(ii) *B*	[1]
(iii) *C*	[1]
(iv) *C*	[1]
(v) *C*	[1]
(vi) *A*	[1]

The key for multiple-choice questions such as these is to **be on high alert for synonyms**. Straight away, Yousef mentions that he wants to take a month to relax (*pour me détendre*), which is a synonym of *prendre une pause*, as seen in **A**.

Be careful: the fact he's travelling with another chef doesn't mean that he's going to cook, as he says he's going *pour gouter les différentes nourritures*. *Un chef* is also another word for a boss, *un patron*, and he also mentions his sister, *ma soeur*, in the recording, which are small traps for **(iii)** as these are options for answers. He says he is going with a chef who is *à la fois mon ami et le mari de ma soeur*, meaning that he is both his friend and the husband of his sister. Similarly, in question **(v)** he mentions both his father and sister, but it was his mother who inspired him.

The expression *je n'y suis jamais allé* means that he has never been before, so we can assume that he is going to see the country (**C**).

Full transcript for Question 5

F1   *Félicitations Yousef, vous devez être très fier d'avoir gagné le prix pour être un des meilleurs chefs de France.*

M1   *Oui, c'est un grand honneur et je n'arrive pas à le croire. J'ai beaucoup travaillé et maintenant **je vais prendre un mois pour me détendre** un peu.*

F1   *Très bien, qu'est-ce que vous allez faire pendant ce mois?*

M1   *Alors, je vais aller faire un tour de l'Inde pour **gouter les différentes nourritures**! J'y vais avec un autre chef, qui est à la fois **mon ami** et le mari de ma sœur. Nous voulons travailler ensemble dans l'avenir. C'est une bonne opportunité pour explorer car **je n'y suis jamais allé**.*

F1   *Ça a toujours été votre inspiration quand vous étiez petit?*

M1   *C'était toujours **ma mère**, elle cuisinait des repas délicieux pour moi et ma sœur. Mon père cuisine bien aussi mais la meilleure, c'était toujours ma mère.*

F1   *Et quel est votre ingrédient secret?*

M1   *La passion, j'adore mon travail et c'est un vrai plaisir de cuisiner pour les autres, surtout pour **partager un bon moment entre amis**, c'est ça la culture de ma famille.*

Mark Scheme:

0-6	- Award one mark for each correct answer, up to six. - If more than one box per question is crossed, then no marks are awarded.

L'argent de Poche

6 Vous allez entendre une interview avec Florent.	
(i) *des petit trucs*	[1]
(ii) *attendre son anniversaire, faire des économies*	[2]
(iii) *des bonbons, des magazines*	[2]
(iv) *la somme a augmenté*	[1]
(v) *il travaille comme serveur*	[1]
(vi) *il a acheté une guitare*	[1]
(vii) *c'est important*	[1]
(viii) *il ne lui inspire pas, les clients sont méchants, c'est fatigant*	[2]

Longer passages like this are designed to help the strongest candidates achieve top grades, and may contain unfamiliar words or terms. If you don't understand something that you hear, **try to work it out from the context.**

For this question, you only need **one or two words**, or a **succinct phrase** (in French) for each answer. **Don't write too much or copy down everything you hear**, as this would imply to the examiner that you haven't understood the task. You need to be selective and work within the timespan, so either **quote carefully**, or **accurately paraphrase** what you hear. Again, you will need to check how much information is needed, as some answers carry two marks.

This interview moves quite quickly so a lot of information may seem relevant to more than one answer. You will need to pick out and identify the answers carefully while listening to whole sentences. **Look out for the clues at the start of the sentences** which tell you what is being referred to. For example, Florent received a small amount of money when he was younger and the phrase *quand j'étais plus jeune* is an indicator for the third question.

Keep an eye out for synonyms here. There are three main ways of saying 'to save money' and they are: *faire des économies*, *économiser* and *mettre de l'argent de côté*.

Full transcript for Question 6

F1 *Alors Florent, recevez-vous de l'argent de poche?*

M1 *Oui, j'ai toujours reçu une somme d'argent, c'est à dire assez pour acheter **des petits trucs que je voulais**. Mais pour les vêtements ou des choses plus chères il faut soit **attendre mon anniversaire** soit **faire des économies**.*

F1 *Est-ce que la somme que vous recevez à changée?*

M1 *Quand j'étais petit je recevais une toute petite somme pour m'acheter **des bonbons** ou **des magazines**. A l'âge de seize ans **la somme a augmenté**. Maintenant j'achète de la musique et récemment j'ai acheté un abonnement pour un site web qui loue des films.*

F1 *Est-ce que vous arrivez à économiser?*

M1 *Un peu. Pour gagner un peu plus, je **travaille comme serveur dans un restaurant** près de chez moi. Je ne gagne pas beaucoup mais j'économise, après quatre mois de travail j'ai pu **m'acheter une guitare**. C'est ma passion.*

F1 *Est-ce que vous aimez travailler?*

M1 *Oui et à mon avis c'est important mais je dois dire que mon boulot **ne m'inspire pas** vraiment! **Les clients sont méchants** et **le travail est fatiguant**.*

F1 *Merci Florent.*

Mark Scheme:

0-11	- Award one mark for each correct answer, up to eleven.
	- Candidate may quote succinctly from the text, or use their own words.
	- Vague answers which indicate guesswork do not score.
	- Overly long answers do not score, as they indicate that the candidate hasn't fully understood the point.

END OF SOLUTIONS FOR PAPER 3

Listening Paper 4

Visit **www.rsleducational.co.uk/frenchaudio** to download the audio file for this paper.

If you wish to complete this paper in timed conditions, allow 40 minutes plus 5 minutes' reading time.

Instructions

- Use **black** ink or ballpoint pen.
- Answer **all** questions.
- Answer the questions in the spaces provided.
  - o *There may be more space than you require.*
- Dictionaries are **not** allowed.

Advice

- You have 5 minutes to read through the paper before the recording starts.
- You will hear each extract twice. You may write at any time during the examination. There will be a pause after each question.
- Read each question **carefully** before attempting it.
- The marks available for each question are given in [square brackets]. These give you an indication of how long to spend on it.
- There is a total of **50 marks** available for this paper.
- Leave time to check your answers at the end, if possible.

Answer ALL questions.

At the doctor's

Écrivez la bonne lettre dans la case.
Write the correct letter in the box.

1   Où ont-ils mal?
        What's wrong with them?

A	A sore throat
B	A stomach ache
C	A headache
D	A sore knee
E	A broken leg
F	A bad back

Pour chaque enregistrement, choisissez la raison pour la visite au médecin et écrivez la bonne lettre dans la case.

For each recording, choose the reason for the doctor's visit and write the correct letter in the box.

(i)	
(ii)	
(iii)	
(iv)	

(Total for Question 1 = 4 marks)

A new shopping centre

Écoutez l'annonce et cochez [X] la bonne lettre pour chaque question.
Listen to the advert and put a cross [X] by the correct letter for each question.

2   Écoutez cette annonce pour un nouveau centre commercial à la radio.
Listen to this advert for a new shopping centre on the radio.

(i)   The centre is...

A	opening this Wednesday at 10am	
B	opening this Tuesday at 9am	
C	opening this Thursday at 8am	

(ii)   The shops available include...

A	make-up shops	
B	hairdressers	
C	perfume shops	

(iii)   If you join for the opening, you get...

A	a discount	
B	a free meal	
C	a free drink	

(Total for Question 2 = 3 marks)

TV Shows

Écoutez l'annonce et cochez [X] la bonne lettre pour chaque question.
Listen to the advert and put a cross [X] by the correct letter for each question.

3a   Écoutez Leila qui parle d'une nouvelle série.
           Listen to Leila who's talking about a new series.

(i)   She thinks it will be popular because...

A	it is available online.	
B	it is interesting.	
C	the plot is good.	

(ii)   She likes watching programmes online because it's...

A	as good as on the television.	
B	better than on the television.	
C	better than last year.	

3b   Écoutez Jean qui parle des séries.
           Listen to Jean who is talking about TV series.

(iii)   He thinks the cinema is...

A	better than watching tv series.	
B	not as good as watching tv series.	
C	not as good as renting DVDs.	

(iv)   He thinks TV shows are...

A	as good as english ones.	
B	dubbed badly in French.	
C	dubbed well in French.	

3c Écoutez Anna qui parle des séries.
Listen to Anna who is talking about TV series.

(v) She thinks TV shows are...

A	a waste of her time.	
B	amusing.	
C	great to watch with her mother.	

(vi) As for Spanish, she thinks that...

A	she needs to learn it.	
B	it is a useful language.	
C	she will study it at school.	

(Total for Question 3 = 6 marks)

Coding in school

Écoutez le reportage et complétez les phrases **en anglais**.
Listen to the report and complete the sentences **in English**.

4   Vous êtes en France et vous écoutez ce reportage qui parle du codage au collège.

You are in France and you hear this report about coding in schools.

Exemple:

In schools, there has been a revolution of **computing education**.
It's important in our lives because we are often **led by technology**.

(i)   This subject has, however, not attracted much ....

(ii)   Following a recent survey, the students were not ....

(iii)   Computing skills are vital to ....

(iv)   Coding is now taught through ....

(Total for Question 4 = 4 marks)

A music festival

Écoutez le reportage et complétez les phrases **en anglais**.
Listen to the report and complete the sentences **in English**.

5   Vous êtes en France et vous écoutez ce reportage qui parle d'un festival de musique au sud de la France.

You are in France and you hear this report about a music festival in the south of France.

Exemple: How often does the festival takes place?
Every two years.

(i)   How long will the festival last this year?   [1]

....

(ii)   How long did the festival last the previous year?   [1]

....

(iii)   What two new places will be used as music venues this year? Give **two** details.   [2]

....

....

(iv)   What two things are not allowed during the festival? Give **two** details.   [2]

....

....

(Total for Question 5 = 6 marks)

Social Media

Écoutez le reportage et notez les détails **en anglais**.
Listen to the report and note the details **in English**.

6   Vous êtes en France et vous écoutez un podcast avec un groupe de jeunes qui parle des avantages et désavantages des réseaux sociaux.

        You are in France and you listen to a podcast with a group of young people who are talking about the advantages and disadvantages of social media.

(i)   **Emma**

Advantage	Disadvantage

(ii)   **Alice**

Advantage	Disadvantage

(Total for Question 6 = 4 marks)

English Language School

Écoutez l'annonce et cochez **[X]** la bonne lettre pour chaque question.
Listen to the advert and put a cross **[X]** by the correct letter for each question.

7   Vous entendez une annonce pour une école de langues en France.
     You hear an advert for a language school in France.

(i)   The advert is aimed at...

A	people who are advanced in French.	
B	people who want to get better in French.	
C	people who failed in their exams.	

(ii)   The classes last...

A	for one week only.	
B	for the whole of a summer.	
C	for one week to a month.	

(iii)   The advert ask that you...

A	are a confident speaker.	
B	are willing to speak.	
C	speak French.	

(iv)   To apply, you need to...

A	download the form.	
B	email the form.	
C	fill in the form online.	

(Total for Question 7 = 4 marks)

Fashion

Écoutez et répondez aux questions suivantes **en anglais**.
Listen and answer the following questions **in English**.

8   Écoutez ces jeunes qui parlent de la mode en France.
          Listen to these young people speak about fashion in France.

(i)   Why doesn't Camille have time to be fashionable? Give **one** detail. [1]

....

(ii) What does Nicolas think about fashion? Give **one** detail.   [1]

....

(iii) Why does Léa like fashion? Give **one** detail.   [1]

....

(Total for Question 8 = 3 marks)

War Orphans

9   Écoutez ce reportage des pupilles de l'état. Cochez [X] la bonne lettre pour chaque question.

Listen to this report about war orphans. Put a cross [X] by the correct letter for each question.

(i)   The law is aimed at...

A	orphaned children.	
B	children orphaned through war or terrorism.	
C	children aged twenty five or younger orphaned through war or terrorism.	

(ii)   They receive...

A	financial and emotional support.	
B	somewhere to live.	
C	counselling .	

(iii)   During the First World War, children...

A	had to apply for government protection.	
B	were granted a specific status.	
C	were given financial aid.	

(iv)   The amount of money given depends on...

A	the individual situation.	
B	the decision of the Ministry of Veterans.	
C	the age of the child.	

(Total for Question 9 = 4 marks)

This Weekend

Cochez [X] les deux phrases qui sont vraies.
Put a cross [X] next to the two sentences which are true.

10   Vous êtes en France et vous écoutez la mère de votre amie qui parle de ce que vous allez faire ce weekend.

You're in France and you listen to your friend's mother speak about what you're going to do this weekend.

A	The grandparents live in the city.	
B	They will visit castles and vineyards.	
C	They will buy a present for the grandparents at the vineyard.	
D	They have tennis rackets at the house.	
E	It will be sunny this weekend.	

(Total for Question 10 = 2 marks)

Footballers

Complétez les phrases suivantes en français.
Complete the following sentences **in French**.

11   Dans un parc en France, vous écoutez des jeunes qui parlent des footballeurs.
In a park in France, you hear some young people talking about footballers.

(i)   Alycia pense que les frais de transferts sont…   [1]

....

(ii)   En protestation, des supporteurs ont… (Donnez **un** détail)   [1]

....

(iii)   Elle pense que le salaire hebdomadaire est trop élevé parce que…   [1]

....

(iv)   Gabrielle pense que le foot… (Donnez **un** détail)   [1]

....

(v)   Elle pense que ces joueurs méritent leur salaire parce que…   [1]

....

(vi)   En ce qui concerne les billets, elle pense que…   [1]

....

(Total for Question 11 = 6 marks)

Healthy Living

Choisissez le conseil mentionné et cochez **[X]** la bonne case.
Choose the advice mentioned and put a cross **[X]** in the correct box.

12   Écoutez ce reportage de gens qui parlent d'une vie saine.
        Listen to this report on people talking about healthy living.

A	Achetez de la nourriture bio.	
B	Menez une vie équilibrée.	
C	Ne mangez pas trop de nourriture grasse.	
D	Mangez rarement les plats préparés.	
E	Buvez assez d'eau.	
F	Dormez pendant huit heures chaque nuit.	
G	Faites de l'exercice régulièrement.	

(Total for Question 12 = 4 marks)

TOTAL FOR PAPER = 50 MARKS

Blank Page

Listening Paper 4 – SOLUTIONS

At the doctors

1 Où ont-ils mal?	
(i) C	[1]
(ii) E	[1]
(iii) A	[1]
(iv) B	[1]

Remember that you have five minutes before the recording to look at the questions. Use some of this time to think what each English phrase would be in French.

In this simple warm-up question, you are required to put the correct letter in each answer box once you hear the relevant French word(s) in the dialogue. Remember to **make notes in the blank space** until you are as certain of your answer as you can be. Neatly cross out each option once you have used it, so you know not to use it again.

Full transcript for Question 1

F1   *Je ne peux plus me concentrer, j'ai trop **mal à la tête**.*

F1   *C'est arrivé pendant un match de foot. Je pense que **je me suis cassé la jambe**.*

F1   *Je n'arrive pas à parler, j'ai **mal à la gorge**.*

F1   *Je pense que j'ai mangé quelque chose de mauvais, j'ai envie de vomir, **j'ai mal au ventre**.*

Mark Scheme:

0-4	- Award one mark for each correct answer, up to four.

A new shopping centre

2 Écoutez cette annonce pour un nouveau centre commercial	
(i) B	[1]
(ii) C	[1]
(iii) A	[1]

In this short extract you are expected to identify the core vocabulary for 'local area' and 'shopping'. There are no tricks: it's just a matter of identifying the correct answer. If you don't know the word for 'discount' **(iii)**, try to work out the words for meal (*repas*) and drink (*boisson*), which will help you to eliminate these answers.

Full transcript for Question 2

M1 *Attention chers clients, le nouveau centre commercial Les Rues de Luxes va ouvrir ses portes **ce mardi à 9 heures**.*
Vous aurez de la chance, il y a quelque chose pour tout le monde, même les animaux.
*Nous avons des restaurants, des magasins de vêtements et **des parfumeries**.*
*Si vous nous rejoignez pour l'ouverture, vous pourrez avoir **un rabais** de vingt pourcent dans tous les magasins.*

Mark Scheme:

0-3	- Award one mark for each correct answer, up to three. - If more than one box per question is crossed, then no marks are awarded.

TV shows

3 Écoutez Leila qui parle d'une nouvelle série.	
(i) C	[1]
(ii) B	[1]
(iii) A	[1]
(iv) B	[1]
(v) B	[1]
(vi) B	[1]

Be careful not to trip up on the first hurdle as you hear *en ligne*. The answer to **(i)** is introduced by *ça va être très populaire partout parce que…*, which will guide you to the correct answer.

As with **Paper 2, Question 6**, make sure you **revise your comparatives and superlatives** so you are able to understand, for example, that she finds watching shows online *mieux qu'à la télé*: better than on TV. Question **(iii)** mentions DVDs, but if you listen to the whole extract you will hear him say that he finds going to the cinema a better experience: *toute l'expérience est meilleure*. For question **(iv)**, you will hear the repetition of his dislike for dubbing. If you don't understand *mal doublé*, you may still get it with *c'est insupportable*.

In Anna's extract, another trap is set as you will hear *une perte de temps*, but this refers to **her mother's opinion** of TV shows. Other people's opinions are often given (which may be relevant to other parts of the question), so it is important to listen attentively.

The final question is a bit tricky. She mentions the fact that she already studies Spanish (**A** is eliminated), but that they don't have enough classes. She needs to get better at it

(**C** is eliminated), as she says *je voudrais améliorer mon espagnol*. We can settle on **B** when she says *c'est utile comme langue*.

Full transcript for Question 3

F 1   *Je viens de regarder en ligne une nouvelle série française. C'est une série policière et je pense que ça va être très populaire parce que **l'histoire est captivante**. J'adore regarder des séries en ligne car **elles sont mieux qu'à la télé**. Il y a plusieurs genres différents et il y a plus en plus d'émissions qui sont disponibles chaque semaine.*

F2   *Alors Jean, qu'est-ce que vous pensez des séries?*

M1   *Je ne les regarde pas. **J'aime** louer des films et surtout **aller au cinéma** car **toute l'expérience est meilleure**. À la télé, il y a trop d'émissions en anglais et ils sont, bien sûr, mal doublées en français et c'est insupportable.*

F2   *Et vous Anna, qu'est-ce que vous aimez?*

F 1   *Moi, je trouve les séries télé vraiment **drôles, divertissantes** et une bonne distraction après l'école à la fin d'une longue journée. Cependant, ma mère n'est pas du tout d'accord et elle pense que je passe trop de temps devant l'écran, que c'est une perte de temps, mais bon. Mes parents ont tort, je peux regarder les séries en ligne en n'importe quelle langue, même en espagnol. Je voudrais améliorer mon espagnol car on n'a pas assez d'heures de cours d'espagnol et **c'est utile comme langue**.*

Mark Scheme:

0-6	- Award one mark for each correct answer, up to six. - If more than one box per question is crossed, then no marks are awarded.

Coding in schools

4 Vous êtes en France et vous écoutez ce reportage.	
(i) *interest*	[1]
(ii) *inspired*	[1]
(iii) *getting a job*	[1]
(iv) *games*	[1]

The recordings get more complex, in terms of the level of French used and the vocabulary, through each paper. When listening to these more complex extracts later in the paper, it's important not to panic and to remember that **you aren't expected to understand every word**. Listen for the words you do understand and piece together the information.

Make sure you allow time to **read the questions beforehand** as they will help guide you through the extract. You will be expected to undestand *ce sujet n'a pas attiré* *assez...*, which leads you into the answer: that the subject hasn't attracted enough interest. Although the language used may be of a high level, the words you are expected to write down are words that you will have seen many times before.

Full transcript for Question 4

F1 *Malgré la révolution de l'éducation informatique dans les dernières années grâce à son importance dans nos vies, souvent dominées par la technologie, ce sujet n'a pas attiré assez **d'intérêt chez les étudiants**. Selon un sondage récent, les étudiants n'étaient pas **inspirés** par le sujet.*

*Les compétences informatiques sont essentielles pour **trouver un emploi** et cela ne va pas changer. Maintenant, pour les jeunes, ils ont introduit beaucoup **de jeux** qui essayent d'enseigner le codage d'une manière divertissante.*

Mark Scheme:

0-4	- Award one mark for each correct answer, up to four. - Vague answers may indicate guesswork and do not score.

A music festival

5 Vous êtes en France et vous écoutez ce reportage.	
(i) *one week*	[1]
(ii) *a weekend*	[1]
(ii) *a street party* **and** *the Palais de la Mer*	[2]
(iii) *don't make too much noise* **and**	
drugs are banned	[2]

This question is very similar to the one before, but relevant pieces of information occur in quick succession, so you will need to note down your ideas more quickly.

The trick for this question is to realise that the usual key phrases may not be present. For question **(ii)**, you may be expecting to hear *l'année dernière* as the questions asks how long the festival lasted 'last year', but here the answer is given in the phrase introduced with *cette année*. The festival this year will last more than a weekend, *cette année on a de la chance car, pour la première fois, le festival va durer plus qu'un weekend*, and we can therefore infer that last year, the festival only lasted a weekend.

For names of places, countries and venues, you don't need to worry too much about the spelling – but aim to be as close as possible. This goes for the *Palais de la Mer*, for example – and **you aren't expected to translate this into English**.

The last question asks for things which aren't allowed during the festival. The first answer is given as a negative construction, *ne pas faire trop de bruit*, but the second is not. The adjective *interdites* is given, meaning 'forbidden'. Don't start with a fixed idea about whether you're looking for a positive or negative phrase.

Full transcript for Question 5

F1   *Ce festival prestigieux a lieu tous les deux ans dans notre ville tranquille, mais cette année on a de la chance car, pour la première fois, le festival va durer plus qu'**un weekend** et on peut célébrer la musique pendant toute **une semaine**. Nous avons encore de bonnes nouvelles car cette année nous aurons deux nouveaux espaces de musique! Le premier est **une fête dans la rue** Marchande et aussi nous pourrons utiliser **le nouveau Palais de la Mer**. Comme d'habitude, les choses suivantes sont interdites pendant le festival: il faut respecter les habitants et ne **pas faire trop de bruit** dans les rues après les concerts. **Les drogues** sont absolument interdites.*

Mark Scheme:

0-6	- Award one mark for each correct answer, up to six. - Vague answers may indicate guesswork and do not score.

Social Media

6 Vous êtes en France et vous écoutez un podcast.	
(i) advantage: *staying in touch with friends*	[1]
disadvantage: *it's a distraction*	[1]
(ii) advantage: *she likes following famous people/stars*	[1]
disadvantage: *she spends too much time on it*	[1]

This is a notorious question type, which many people find challenging! You need to identify positive and negative opinions. The first speaker says that social media is good (*excellents*) to stay in touch with family; but that she also finds it a distraction when working (*une grande distraction*). The question is testing your ability to understand each opinion and note it down in English. You don't need to translate exactly that is being said: you need to show that you have understood the opinion.

Full transcript for Question 6

F1   *Emma, vous avez déménagé ici, qu'est-ce que vous pensez des réseaux sociaux?*
F2   *Pour moi, ils sont excellents pour **rester en contact avec mes amis** mais **c'est aussi une grande distraction quand il faut travailler**.*
F1   *Et vous, Alice, qu'en pensez-vous?*

F2   *J'aime bien **suivre les vedettes** que j'admire mais **je passe trop de temps** à les regarder.*

Mark Scheme:

0-4	- Award one mark for each correct answer, up to four. Your answers needn't be identical to the examples above. - Vague answers may indicate guesswork and do not score.

English Language School

7 Vous entendez une annonce pour une école de langues en France.	
(i) *B*	[1]
(ii) *C*	[1]
(ii) *B*	[1]
(iii) *A*	[1]

In question **(ii)** you will hear *pendant les grandes vacances*, which means 'during the summer holidays' (suggesting **B**), but also that the courses last from one week to a month: *d'une semaine à un mois*.

Try to annotate the answers by **writing down some words in French which you might expect to hear**. For **(iv)** you may be looking for the word 'download', *télécharger*, 'email', *couriel*, or 'fill in the form' (*remplir la fiche*). If you don't have time to note this down, then the best thing is to think of what the words in the question are in French. When you hear the word *télécharger*, you can quickly tick the box.

Full transcript for Question 7

F1   *Vous voulez réussir vos examens? Vous avez reçu de mauvaises notes? Ou **voulez-vous simplement améliorer votre niveau**? Ne vous inquiétez pas, nous dirigeons une école de langues dans le centre de Clermont-Ferrand. Nous avons des programmes de cours qui durent **entre une semaine et un mois** pendant les grandes vacances.*

*La seule chose que nous voulons, c'est que **vous veniez avec beaucoup d'enthousiasme pour parler cette nouvelle langue**. Vous pouvez aller sur notre site web pour **télécharger le formulaire de candidature**.*

Mark Scheme:

0-4	- Award one mark for each correct answer, up to four.
	- If more than one box per question is crossed, then no marks are awarded.

Fashion

8 Écoutez ces jeunes qui parlent de la mode en France.	
(i) *You have to be on all the blogs* **or** *know all the brands*	[1]
(ii) *Fashion doesn't exist* **or** *it forces us to spend money*	[1]
(ii) *It's an expression of her personality* **or** *she loves to experiment*	[1]

You don't need to write in full sentences as you won't have time for that: just note down as much as you can. For example, in question **(ii)**, Nicolas says *la mode n'existe pas. Ce n'est qu'une manière de nous forcer d'acheter plus*. You could simply write, 'fashion doesn't exist' or 'it forces us to buy things'. The main thing is to show your understanding of the dialogue.

Full transcript for Question 8

F1 *Je m'appelle Camille et je n'ai vraiment pas assez de temps pour être à la mode. **Il faut être sur tous les blogs** et **connaître chaque marque**. En plus, les vêtements de marque sont très chers.*

M1 *Je suis Nicolas et à mon avis **la mode n'existe pas. Ce n'est qu'une manière de nous forcer d'acheter plus**. Nous vivons dans un monde de consommateur et moi, je préfère l'ignorer.*

F2 *Je m'appelle Léa et j'aime beaucoup m'habiller car je le vois comme **une expression de ma personnalité** et **j'adore expérimenter** avec des couleurs et des textures.*

Mark Scheme:

0-3	- Award one mark for each correct answer, up to three.
	- Vague answers may indicate guesswork and do not score.

War Orphans

9 Écoutez ce reportage des pupilles de l'état.	
(i) *B*	[1]
(ii) *A*	[1]
(iii) *B*	[1]
(iv) *A*	[1]

With a tricky topic such as this, make sure you **read all the instructions**. The title is in English and then you are given the question in both French and English. The vocabulary *pupilles de l'état* , 'war orphans', is not something which you would be expected to know in French – which is why it is there in English in the question.

This question requires a detailed understanding. For question **(i)**, **A** is a possibility as the law is aimed at children who have been orphaned, but the key information, that it's aimed at children who have been orphaned *en consequence d'une guerre ou un acte terroriste*, is **B**. **C** mentions children and young people under the age of twenty one, *les jeunes moins de vingt et un ans*, not twenty five, so it cannot be the answer.

As with all multiple-choice questions, try and **read as much as possible before the recording starts** as the English will help you through the tricky spoken text.

Full transcript for Question 9

M1   *Suite aux attentats en France ces dernières années, il y maintenant plusieurs enfants qui sont devenus orphelins. Il y a une loi, qui n'est pas très bien connue, pour **les enfants ou les jeunes de moins de vingt et un ans dont les parents ont été tués à cause d'une guerre ou d'un acte terroriste.** Ces orphelins peuvent être « adoptés par la nation » et ils deviennent pupilles de la nation.*

*Ils pourront bénéficier **d'un soutien financier et moral** qui inclue un financement de leurs études, de l'aide pour trouver leur premier emploi et des cadeaux de Noël. Cette loi date de la première guerre mondiale quand environ un million **d'enfants ont reçus ce statut précis** qui leur a garantis une protection. La somme d'argent donnée aux enfants **est spécifique à leur situation**, celle-ci est décidée par le ministère des anciens combattants et des victimes de la guerre.*

Mark Scheme:

0-4	- Award one mark for each correct answer, up to four. - If more than one box per question is crossed, then no marks are awarded.

This weekend

10   Vous êtes en France et vous écoutez la mère de votre ami
B **and** E   [2]

The answer cannot be **A** as your friend's mother says her parents live in the countryside, *à la campagne*. She goes on to say that they will pass castles and vineyards, *de châteaux et des vignobles*, so you can cross **B** as a correct answer. She does mention the buying of a present, but in this case it is for your parents, not the grandparents: *nous pourrions acheter un cadeau pour tes parents*. She says to bring tennis rackets, *il faut amener ta raquette* so we can eliminate **D** and that leaves us with **E**.

Full transcript for Question 10

F1   *Ce weekend nous sommes invités chez mes parents qui habitent à la campagne. On va y passer deux jours et c'est un endroit très tranquille. Le trajet dure deux heures mais on **va passer devant plusieurs sites historiques que nous pourrons visiter comme des châteaux et des vignobles** où peut-être nous pourrions acheter un cadeau pour tes parents. Mes parents ont un terrain de tennis et une piscine donc il faut amener ta raquette et ton maillot de bain. **Il va faire très, très chaud** donc n'oublie pas la crème solaire.*

Mark Scheme:

0-2	- Award one mark for each correct answer, up to two.
	- If more than two boxes are crossed, then no marks are awarded.

Footballers

11 **Dans un parc en France, vous écoutez des jeunes qui parlent des footballeurs.**	
(i) *trop chers*	[1]
(ii) *ils ont quittés le stade* **or** *ils ont jeté des balles de tennis sur le terrain*	[1]
(iii) *les billets sont trop chers*	[1]
(iv) *le sport le plus populaire* **or** *il génère beaucoup d'argent*	[1]
(v) *ils sont les meilleurs au monde*	[1]
(vi) *il y a toujours assez de gens qui vont payer*	[1]

The final questions in an exam are designed to test the strongest GCSE candidates and are deliberately tricky. In this question, you are asked to respond in French. **Take notes and then write your answers during a pause in the recording.**

You must change the grammar to make it appropriate for the answer. For the first question, Alycia says a transfer is too expensive, *c'est vraiment trop*. Question **(i)** is asking for an answer in the plural as the nouns and verb are in the plural, *les frais de transferts sont...*: you can simply change your answer to *trop chers*. Your sentences need to be **as gramatically accurate as possible**.

For question **(vi)** you want to get across the opinion that there will always be people who will pay top prices for the tickets, so you could write that *les gens vont toujours payer* or *il y a toujours assez de gens qui vont payer*.

Full transcript for Question 11

M1 *Alycia que penses-tu de Paul Pogba?*

F1 *Je l'adore mais cent-million d'euros pour un transfert? À mon avis **c'est vraiment trop** et je ne suis pas la seule à penser ça. Tu te rappelles, des supporters **ont quittés le stade** en protestation et **ils ont même jeté des balles de tennis sur le terrain**. Moi, je ne peux pas comprendre le salaire d'un quart de million chaque semaine pour un joueur. Et nous, **nous payons un prix fou pour les billets**.*

M1 *Et vous Gabrielle?*

F2 *Ben, le foot c'est **le sport le plus populaire au monde** et **il génère beaucoup d'argent**. **Ces joueurs sont les meilleurs au monde** et donc ils méritent ce salaire important. La saison dernière, quatre-vingt-quinze pourcent des billets étaient vendus donc **il y a toujours ceux qui sont prêts à payer le prix**.*

Mark Scheme:

0-6	- Award one mark for each correct answer, up to six. - Vague answers may indicate guesswork and do not score. - If grammatical errors hinder understanding, that answer will not gain a mark.

Healthy Living

12 Écoutez ce reportage de gens qui parlent d'une vie saine.	
(i) *B*	[1]
(ii) *C*	[1]
(iii) *E*	[1]
(iv) *G*	[1]

This question is similar to **Question 10**, the only real difference being the increase in difficulty. Cross off the answers you can eliminate as you go. There are slight differences between the words you are looking for and the words in the question. **B** is expressed in the answer as maintaining a good balance, *mainternir un bon équilibre*, which matches the statement with the advice to lead a balanced life, *menez une vie équilibrée*. **C** advises not to eat too many fatty foods and we can find the answer in *il faut...réduire notre consummation d'aliments gras*, which means 'we must... reduce our consumption of fatty foods'.

The answers rely on your full comprehension of the extract, so make sure you listen to the whole text carefully.

Full transcript for Question 12

F2　　*Bonjour et bienvenu à notre reportage, aujourd'hui nous allons discuter de la vie saine. Qu'est-ce qu'on peut faire pour changer nos habitudes?*

M1　　*Selon moi, il ne faut pas devenir obsédé par le bien-être mais essayer de **maintenir un bon équilibre**. Evidemment, il faut toujours manger une grande quantité de légumes et **réduire notre consommation d'aliments gras**.*

F1　　*À mon avis, il faut toujours éviter les plats préparés car ils sont remplis de conservateurs. **Nous avons besoin de boire huit verres d'eau** chaque jour et le sommeil est important aussi. Finalement, il est nécessaire de bouger! Il faut essayer de **faire de l'exercice trois fois par semaine**.*

Mark Scheme:

0-4	- Award one mark for each correct answer, up to four. - If more than four boxes are crossed, then no marks are awarded.

END OF SOLUTIONS FOR PAPER 4

Oral (Speaking) Primer

Visit **www.rsleducational.co.uk/frenchaudio** to download the conversation recordings discussed in this guide.

The recordings demonstrate how to approach the oral examinations in French and feature a genuine GCSE student. They cover the **conversation** section of the oral exam. This is the part that many students fear most, and may not know how to prepare for properly.

This section of the pack explains how to improve your grade in this part of the exam and also provides marking grids.

According to the exam board you are with, other sections of the oral exam may include a role play, a short topic presentation (with follow-up questions from the examiner) and/or a picture-based task with follow-up questions or discussion. Some boards use a mixture of these.

Exams involving role-play and/or presentation sections are best prepared for by revising the conversation topics below, making sure you have learnt topic-specific vocabulary and expressions. You can also use the **example questions on pages 115-6** for this purpose.

Mark Scheme

There are three grids to be applied to the general conversation section: communication, interaction and spontaneity, and linguistic knowledge and accuracy.

There are a total of **39 marks** available in this mark scheme, which is **suitable for all exam boards** and can be used by all students.

The breakdown of the **Communication** section looks like this:

Communication

0	- No rewardable material as no information is communicated.
1-3	- Candidate communicates a few relevant facts with short responses. - Candidate finds it difficult to understand the questions. - Candidate has difficulty replying to the questions.
4-6	- Candidate is able to understand straightforward questions. - Candidate finds it difficult to understand more complex questions. - Candidate communicates most elements required with simple opinions and occasional extended responses.
7-9	- Candidate is able to understand straightforward questions with no difficulty and responds well to more complex questions. - Candidate is able to expand on questions and information is usually conveyed clearly. - Candidate communicates all elements required and uses justifications for opinions.
10-12	- Candidate is able to understand and respond to straightforward questions, as well as complex questions, with ease. Occasional rephrasing may be required. - Candidate expands on all questions, develops opinions with justification and information is always conveyed clearly.
13-15	- Candidate consistently responds to all questions with spontaneity and developed responses in a natural conversational exchange. - There is consistency in speaking, though this need not be of native speaker standard, and information is conveyed clearly at all times with opinions and justifications.

In other words, you are required to use language **creatively** to convey your ideas and experiences. Use as much topic-specific vocabulary as you can, as well as interesting expressions. For help with this, see my *Steps to a Higher Grade* document (**page 117**), and use it as a stimulus to come up with ideas of your own as well.

Mistakes are not the end of the world, and perfection is not expected at GCSE level, so be **bold** with your answers and try not to give just the bare minimum response. Instead, look to **extend** your sentences with conjunctions such as *parce que, cependant, en plus*, etc. You can also **link** various ideas with *aussi, d'un côté, d'un autre côté/de l'autre, par contre, bien que (+ subj)* etc. in order to get your point across in an **interesting and convincing** way.

Finally, practice makes perfect! Practise with friends, teachers and others to gain confidence, as well as working on your French accent so that everything you say can be understood.

Next, let's see the breakdown for the **Interaction and Spontaneity** section:

Interaction and spontaneity

0	- No rewardable material
1-3	- Candidate only occasionally responds spontaneously and is often stilted, but with some examples of natural interaction. - Candidate often responds with rehearsed language, irrelevant to the question. - Candidate occasionally sustains communication, with frequent hesitation.
4-6	- Candidate responds spontaneously to some questions, with natural interaction for parts of the conversation. - Candidate initiates and independently develops the conversation sometimes, with some prompting needed. - Candidate sometimes sustains communication, sometimes with rephrasing, self-correction or repairing phrases, but with some hesitation.
7-9	- Candidate responds spontaneously to most questions, with natural interaction for most parts of the conversation. - Candidate mostly initiates and independently develops the conversation. - Candidate sustains communication throughout most of the conversation, sometimes with rephrasing, self-correction or repairing phrases if needed, and with occasional hesitation. - Candidate demonstrates good pronunciation.
10-12	- Candidate responds spontaneously and with ease to questions, resulting in natural interaction throughout. - Candidate consistently initiates and independently develops the conversation. - Candidate sustains communication throughout, rephrasing or using repair strategies if necessary to continue the flow, with minimal hesitation. - Candidate demonstrates very good pronunciation, intonation and fluency. This need not be of native speaker standard.

Again, your answers don't have to be perfect: the exam is intended to mimic a real-life conversation and has to sound **natural** and **spontaneous**. Therefore, a bit of hesitation and pausing is to be expected. Likewise, don't rush through your answers at break-neck speed, as this sounds unnatural. Do, however, respond promptly to the question.

You are also expected to **help the conversation along,** and develop it. So **add in your own ideas** and **lead the discussion** towards issues that you know how to talk about. In this way, you can guide your examiner to questions you have practised. Try not to just give the bare minimum response!

If you do make a mistake, or need a bit more time to understand the question, you can ask your examiner with **repair phrases**, such as those below. Make sure to keep speaking in French, though – **never** revert to English or another language! This way you can still convey your answer, even when you are struggling. For example:

Pourriez-vous répéter la question, s'il vous plaît? = Please can you repeat the question?
Pourriez-vous répéter la question plus doucement, s'il vous plaît? = Can you say the question again more slowly?
Qu'est-ce que vous avez dit? = What did you say?
C'est une question difficile/intéressante! = It's a difficult/interesting question!
Je n'ai jamais pensé à ça avant, mais... = I have never thought about that before, but...
Ce que je veux dire, c'est que... = What I mean to say is...
Je veux dire... = I mean (when self-correcting)...
J'ai commis une erreur = I said that by mistake

Try not to rely on these phrases, but you can use them if you are struggling and need a bit of help or time to think.

Finally, the breakdown for **Linguistic Knowledge and Accuracy**:

Linguistic Knowledge and Accuracy

0	- No rewardable material
1-3	- Candidate manipulates a limited variety of mainly straightforward grammatical structures, with minimal use of complex structures and vocabulary. - Candidate uses some accurate grammatical structures and some successful past, present and future tense conjugations, although with some ambiguity. - Candidate sustains sequences of coherent speech, although errors often hinder clarity of communication and meaning.
4-6	- Candidate demonstrates a variety of straightforward grammatical structures, with some occasional use of complex structures, although with frequent repetition. - Candidate uses generally accurate grammatical structures, and generally successful past, present and future tense conjugations. - Candidate sustains generally coherent speech, although with errors that sometimes hinder clarity of communication and meaning.
7-9	- Candidate manipulates a variety of grammatical structures, with some variety of complex structures. - Candidate uses predominately accurate grammatical structures and mostly successful past, present and future tense conjugations. - Candidate sustains predominately coherent speech, with errors rarely hindering clarity of communication and meaning.
10-12	- Candidate manipulates a wide variety of grammatical structures, with frequent use of complex structures. - Candidate uses consistently accurate grammatical structures, and consistently successful past, present and future tense conjugations. - Candidate sustains fully coherent speech, with errors not hindering clarity of communication and meaning.

Therefore, try and use complex structures in your responses. Use the *Steps to a Higher Grade* document to help with this: fill it in with some of your own ideas too.

You are expected to attempt to use longer sentences, with a range of parts of speech, such as pronouns, conjunctions, adverbs and adjectives, and to **avoid repetition** where possible. Also, you must try and provide a range of tenses when prompted: if the question is about your future plans, you must answer with the future tense; if it is about your past experiences, you must answer in the past!

Even this section of the mark scheme, which focuses on accuracy of language, <u>does not require error-free French</u>! Nevertheless, any errors must not get in the way of your meaning. You can come back and self-correct if you like, or rephrase what you are trying to say. Incorrect gender or adjectival agreements aren't major, mark-losing errors. However, using the incorrect **person** or **tense** with a verb can often be confusing to the examiner and will be penalised. Also, make sure you answer the question you are asked – talking about something unrelated will be construed as a mistake!

To sum up:

There are three **golden rules** for the oral exam. These are similar to the best approach to the long writing question at the end of each reading/writing paper in **Volume 2**:

- ✓ Use **past, present and future** tenses, including with irregular verbs.

- ✓ **Justify** your opinions.

- ✓ **Don't be boring**! Use interesting vocabulary and a wide variety of structures, with minimal repetition.

The Recordings

Now, listen to the recordings of a real GCSE student (see **www.rsleducational.co.uk/frenchaudio**). They cover **three** conversation topics, though in your exam you will probably only have time for two – or perhaps even one, if your answers are detailed enough! The marks I have given each recording are quite severe, for the sake of highlighting the strengths and weaknesses of the different approaches taken.

Recording – Topic Area A: Home and Abroad

In this conversation, the student does very well in using justified responses and interesting vocabulary. Her linguistic structures are mainly correct and she uses the appropriate tense when responding to the questions. There are a few grammatical and pronunciation mistakes but, on the whole, these do not make her answer incomprehensible to a native speaker, and so these are considered minor errors. There is little hesitation in her answers and she always responds to the question accurately and promptly.

Communication	14
Spontaneity/Interaction	11
Linguistic Knowledge/Accuracy	11
Total (Out of 39)	36

Recording – Topic Area B: Education and Employment

In this recording, the student gives slightly shorter responses. She has a high level of vocabulary and uses some complex structures, such as *ça me détend*. Although she tends to give two justifications for her statements, she could have increased her fluency by using conjunctions to link these opinions. Another way to raise her mark would have been to expand on her answers, rather than being prompted. The standard of her responses is consistently very high and she uses the future and perfect tenses.

Communication	13
Spontaneity/Interaction	10
Linguistic Knowledge/Accuracy	10
Total (Out of 39)	**33**

Recording – Topic Area D: The Modern World and the Environment

This is a tricky section but the student has prepared her answers well so that she has something to say on the environment. Her vocabulary is varied and of a high level and she demonstrates few errors in pronunciation and grammar. However, the answers are short and the student could have developed these further to add to the spontaneity of the conversation.

Communication	14
Spontaneity/Interaction	10
Linguistic Knowledge/Accuracy	10
Total (Out of 39)	**34**

Example questions

The following list is not exhaustive, but it demonstrates the standard range of questions that is most likely to be asked by your teacher/examiner.

The questions are designed to test your vocabulary and your ability to express and justify your opinions, as well as your ability to use the present, past, and future tenses when appropriate. Use them to practise!

Topic Area A – Home and Abroad

> Décris-moi où tu habites.
> Comment est le climat?
> Qu'est-ce qu'on peut faire dans ta région?
> Quels sont les avantages et les inconvénients de ta région?
> Quels sont les avantages d'habiter en ville ou à la campagne?
> Où est-ce que tu aimes passer les vacances?
> Où es-tu allé(e) en vacances l'année dernière?
> Comment est-ce que tu vas passer les grandes vacances cette année?
> Quelles seraient tes vacances idéales?
> Est-ce que tu préfères aller en vacances avec ta famille ou avec tes amis? Pourquoi?

Topic Area B – Education and Employment

> Tu étudies quelles matières?
> Qu'est-ce que tu préfères comme matière? Pourquoi?
> Est-ce qu'il y a des matières que tu n'aimes pas?
> Est-ce que tu es sportif/sportive?
> Qu'est-ce que tu fais comme sport?
> Faits-tu partie de l'orchestre/de la chorale au collège?
> Décris-moi ton uniforme scolaire.
> Est-ce que tu aimes l'uniforme de l'école?
> Est-ce que les devoirs sont importants?
> Est-ce que tu penses que c'est important de faire un stage?

Topic Area C – House, Home and Daily Routine

- Décris-moi ta famille?
- Est-ce que tu t'entends bien avec ta famille?
- Parle-moi d'une journée typique pour toi.
- Qu'est-ce que tu fais avec tes amis?
- Qu'est-ce que tu fais pour aider à la maison ?
- Qu'est-ce que tu as fait le weekend dernier?
- Quel est ton repas préféré?
- Parle-moi de la dernière fois que tu es allée au restaurant.
- Qu'est-ce que tu portes normalement, le weekend?
- Quel est ton jour préféré et pourquoi?

Topic Area D – The Modern World and the Environment

- Quel est le problème le plus grave concernant l'environnement?
- Qu'est-ce que ton école fait pour protéger l'environnement?
- Qu'est-ce que tu fais pour protéger l'environnement?
- Qu'est-ce que tu as fait récemment pour aider quelqu'un d'autre?
- Les jeunes d'aujourd'hui regardent trop de télévision. Qu'en penses-tu?
- Les actualités, pourquoi sont-elles importantes?
- Est-ce que tu passes trop de temps sur ton portable ou ton ordinateur?
- Quels sont les avantages et les inconvénients d'Internet?
- Est-ce que tu es déjà allé(e) au théâtre?
- Tu préfères voir les films à la télé ou au cinéma?

Topic Area E – Social Activities, Fitness and Health

- Quelle est ta fête préférée?
- Parle-moi d'une occasion spéciale que tu as fêtée en famille.
- Comment vas-tu fêter ton prochain anniversaire?
- Qu'est-ce que tu fais pendant ton temps libre?
- Est-ce que tu reçois de l'argent de poche?
- Qu'est-ce que tu aimes comme musique?
- Qu'est-ce que tu aimes comme sport?
- Qu'est-ce que tu fais pour rester en forme?
- Décris-moi ton weekend idéal, qu'est-ce que tu ferais?
- Qu'est-ce que tu penses de l'alcool et les drogues?

Steps to a Higher Grade

How to boost your written and oral responses

Below are tips for raising the grade of your written and oral papers. Try and incorporate several of these tenses and structures into each piece of work. Meanwhile, prepare a checklist of things that you often get wrong and quickly write it out at the top of the exam paper before you start. This way you will know what to look for when you check your answers.

Revise all tenses! Even when you are writing in the present tense, there can be some tricky things:

> ➤ Irregular verbs (in all tenses)
> ➤ Verbs with spelling changes, e.g. *jeter – je jette*
> ➤ Verbs with accent changes, e.g. *acheter – j'achète*
> ➤ Verbs taking *à* or *de* directly after them
> ➤ Reflexive verbs (and in the negative)
> ➤ The imperative (for orders and instructions)

The tenses and structures in the list below are particularly useful for a strong performance at GCSE. Be sure to revise them, and to use them whenever you have the opportunity.

1. Past tenses and when to use them

a) Passé Composé

Use the passé composé:

> ✓ To describe a completed action in the past.

Hier, j'ai lavé la voiture.
Yesterday, I washed the car.

> ✓ To describe an event that happened a specific number of times.

Je suis allé(e) trois fois au musée.
I went to the museum three times.

Common misuses:

- Not using *être* verbs with 'house' verbs/DR & MRS VANDERTRAMP* and reflexives.

---

*The following verbs form the mnemonic **DR & MRS VANDERTRAMP**, to help you remember which verbs take *être* in the passé composé.

Descendre	Sortir	Devenir	Rentrer
Rester	Venir	Entrer	Arriver
Monter	Aller	Revenir	Mourir
Retourner	Naître	Tomber	Partir

     ✗   *J'ai parti.*   ✓   *Je suis parti(e).*

     ✗   *Je m'ai lavé.*   ✓   *Je me suis lavé(e).*

- Forgetting verb agreements when using *être*

     ✗   *Elles sont allé.*   ✓   *Elles sont allées.*

     ✗   *Nous nous sommes levé.*   ✓   *Nous nous sommes levés.*

- Forgetting the auxiliary (*avoir* or *être*) verb.

     ✗   *Je mangé.*   ✓   *J'ai mangé.*

b) Imperfect Tense

Use the imperfect tense:

   ✓   To describe an interrupted action in the past.

<u>*Je regardais la télé*</u> *quand ma mère est entrée.*
I was watching TV when my Mum came in.

   ✓   To describe an incomplete action in the past, i.e. we don't know when or if the event ended.

J'étais en France.
I was in France.

Je préparais le diner.
I was making dinner.

   ✓   For description in the past.

Il faisait beau.
It was sunny.

✓ To describe how people felt in the past.

J'étais triste.
I was sad.

    ✓ To say what 'used to' happen.

Je nageais chaque semaine.
I used to swim every week.

    ✓ To express a habitual or repeated action in the past.

Je visitais ma grand-mère le samedi.
I used to visit my grandmother on Saturdays.

Key points:

- Verbs ending in *–cer* and *–ger* change to:

c to *ç*	*commencer*	*je commençais*
g to *ge*	*manger*	*je mangeais*

- *Être* is the only irregular verb in the imperfect tense.

c) Pluperfect tense

Use the pluperfect tense:

    ✓ To describe something that 'had' happened.

J'avais déjà fini mes devoirs.
I had already finished my homework.

    ✓ With the imperfect tense of *avoir* or *être* + the past participle.

Use the table below to see the simple formation of the compound tenses with the auxiliary verbs:

AVOIR			
In the present for passé composé	*In imperfect for pluperfect*	*In conditional for conditional perfect*	
J'ai	J'avais	J'aurais	**+**
Tu as	Tu avais	Tu aurais	**past participle**
Il/Elle/On a	Il/Elle/On avait	Il/Elle/On aurait	
Nous avons	Nouse avions	Nous aurions	
Vous avez	Vous aviez	Vous auriez	
Ils/Elles ont	Ils/Elles avaient	Ils/Elles auraient	
ÊTRE			
In the present for passé composé	*In imperfect for pluperfect*	*In conditional for conditional perfect*	
Je suis	J'étais	Je serais	**+**
Tu es	Tu étais	Tu serais	**past participle**
Il/Elle/On est	Il/Elle/On était	Il/Elle/On serait	**(Remember**
Nous sommes	Nous étions	Nous serions	**agreements!)**
Vous êtes	Vous étiez	Vous seriez	
Ils/Elles sont	Ils/Elles étaient	Ils/Elles seraient	

The translation of these tenses is as follows:

Passé composé	*J'ai parlé*	I **have** spoken / I spoke
Pluperfect	*J'avais parlé*	I **had** spoken
Conditional perfect	*J'aurais parlé*	I **would have** spoken

2. Future tenses and when to use them

a) The near future tense

Use the near future:

✓ To describe what is going to happen, using *aller* + infinitive.

Je vais faire mes devoirs.
I'm going to do my homework.

b) The simple future tense

Use the future:

✓ To describe what will happen, using the infinitive plus endings*.

Je ferai mes devoirs.
I will do my homework.

*Note that the endings of the simple future are very similar to the present tense of *avoir*:

Avoir	Future tense endings
ai	-ai
as	-as
a	-a
avons	-ons
avez	-ez
ont	-ont

3. The conditional tense and when to use it

Use the conditional:

✓ To describe what **would** happen, using the same stem as the future, + endings*.

Je ferais mes devoirs.
I would do my homework.

*Note that the conditional tense endings are the same as the imperfect tense endings.

Use a website, such as https://leconjugueur.lefigaro.fr/, to look up verbs.

4. Expressing and justifying opinions

By saying **why** you like or dislike something, you will be developing your sentences into more complex, more interesting structures.

a) Expressing opinions

Try to express opinions in your writing and your oral work. Use any of the following to introduce your point of view:

Je pense que…	I think that…
Je trouve que…	I find that…
Il me semble que…	It seems to me that
Je crois que…	I believe that…
J'estime que…	I reckon that…
À mon avis…	In my opinion…
C'est…	It is…
C'était…	It was…
J'ai horreur de…	I hate…
Selon moi…	In my opinion…

b) Justifying opinions

Try to avoid always using *parce que* when giving a justification. In particular, don't overuse the phrase *parce que c'est intéressant*! Instead, look for opportunities to use one of the below, followed by an adjective from section **6(a)**:

car…	because…
puisque…	since…
comme…	as…

5. Use a variety of structures and vocabulary

a) Verbs which take infinitives

The following verbs take infinitives, forming two-verb constructions:
pouvoir / espérer / aimer / devoir / vouloir / savoir / commencer à / décider de

Je peux chanter.	I can sing.
Je veux danser.	I want to dance.
J'ai décidé de réviser.	I decided to revise.

b) Time expressions

✓ Before

Avant de + infinitive

J'ai mangé mon petit déjeuner avant d'aller au collège.
I ate my breakfast before going to school.

✓ After

Après avoir / être + past participle

Après avoir quitté le cinéma, j'ai pris le bus.
After leaving the cinema, I took the bus.

Après être sorti(e) de la maison, je me suis rendu(e) compte que j'avais oublié mon portable.
After leaving the house, I realised I had forgotten my mobile.

✓ For + Time

Pour = expression relates to event happening in the future.

Elle partira pour trois jours.
She'll be away for three days.

Depuis + present tense*

Je joue du piano depuis cinq ans.
I have been playing the piano for five years.

*Depuis makes the sentence sound like the past tense in English, but in French it still has to take the present tense.

Pendant = expression relates to entire duration of an event in past or future.

Nous avons voyagé pendant deux semaines.
We travelled for two weeks.

✓ *An* or *année* / *jour* or *journée*?

Use *an* with <u>cardinal numbers</u>

J'habite à Paris depuis un an.
I have been living in Paris for a year.

Use *année* with <u>ordinal numbers,</u> <u>indefinite adjectives</u> and when one wants to <u>emphasise the length of time.</u>

Elle est en troisième année.
She is in the third year.

Je vais aller à l'université dans quelques années.
I will go to university in a few years.

✓ Useful time expressions

Après-demain	The day after tomorrow	*De temps en temps*	From time to time
Avant-hier	The day before yesterday	*Quelquefois*	Sometimes
À l'avenir	In the future	*Tous les soirs*	Every evening
Bientôt	Soon	*Tous les jours*	Every day
Pendant	During	*Toujours*	Always
D'abord	Firstly	*Souvent*	Often
Enfin	Finally	*Généralement*	Generally, usually
Finalement	Finally	*Normalement*	Normally
Àpres-midi	Afternoon	*D'habitude*	Usually
Hier	Yesterday	*Rarement*	Rarely
Maintenant	Now	*Le mois dernier*	Last month
Demain	Tomorrow	*Parfois*	Sometimes

c) 'Si' clauses

Si means 'if', so these phrases are extremely useful as they allow you to use more than one tense in a sentence and really show off what you can do. See **Section 1** above for a guide to forming the perfect tenses.

Si + Present	Future	*S'il pleut, j'irai au parc.* If it rains, I'll go to the park.
Si + Imperfect	Conditional	*Si j'étais riche, j'achèterais une voiture.* If I were rich, I would buy a car.
Si + Pluperfect	Past conditional	*Si je t'avais vu, j'aurais dit bonjour.* If I had seen you, I would have said hello.

d) Connectives

Alors	So, therefore	*Par exemple*	For example
Puis	Then	*Ensuite*	Then, next
Où	Where	*Donc*	So, therefore
Tandis que	Whereas	*Aussi*	Also
En plus	What's more	*Ainsi*	Thus
Y compris	Including	*Ainsi que*	As well as
Cependant	However	*Mais*	But
Pourtant	However	*Même si*	Even if
Puisque	Since	*Pendant que*	While
Ce que	What	*Au moment*	Just as
Lorsque	When	*Ceci dit*	That said
Pour + infinitive	In order to	*Afin de* + infinitive	In order to

e) Expressions of quantity

The phrase *beaucoup de* is used frequently in French, but try to vary your sentences: you won't achieve excellent marks if you repeat vocabulary.

Quelques + noun	A few
Des + noun	Some
Plusieurs + noun	Several
Beaucoup de + noun*	A lot of
Trop de + noun	Too many
Assez de + noun	Enough of
Autant de + noun	As much, as many
La plupart de + noun	The majority of
La majorité de + noun	The majority of
Encore de + noun	More
Tant de + noun	So much, many
Un peu de + noun	A little bit of

*Don't forget that when expressions of quantity are followed by *de*, the *de* never agrees with the noun, e.g:

*J'ai un kilo **de** pommes.*
I have a kilo of apples.
*J'ai vu beaucoup **d'**animaux.*
I saw a lot of animals.

f) Il y a

✓ **There is / There are**

Il y a quatre stylos dans ma trousse.   **There are** four pens in my pencil case.
Il y avait douze élèves dans ma classe.   **There were** twelve students in my class.
Il y aura une fête cet été.   **There will be** a party this summer.

✓ **Ago**

Je suis allé en France il y a deux ans.
I went to France two years **ago.**

g) *Venir de* + infinitive

✓ *Venir de* means 'to have just done something'

Je viens de passer un weekend en Ecosse.
I have just spent a weekend in Scotland.

Je viens de réussir* mes examens.
I have just passed my exams.

*Remember that 'to pass an exam' is *resussir un examen* and not *passer un examen.*

6. Don't be boring!

It's vital to keep your answers as interesting as possible and in order to do this, you'll need to vary your adjectives and adverbs.

a) Vary your adjectives

Note down as many interesting adjectives that you come across as possible. Below are some examples which you might want to use in your Oral and Writing exams. Try varying your responses with phrases such as *c'était passionant!*

Génial	Great, amazing	*Triste*	Sad
Passionant	Exciting	*Désagréable*	Unpleasant
Marrant	Fun	*Étrange*	Weird
Drôle	Funny	*Ennuyeux*	Boring
Difficile	Difficult	*Fantastique*	Fantastic
Merveilleux	Marvellous	*Méchant*	Nasty
Effrayant	Scary	*Affreux*	Awful

Make sure your adjectives agree!

   ✗ *Ma sœur était content/heureux.*   ✓ *Ma sœur était conte**nte**/heure**use**.*

b) Don't use *très* for everything

Here are some alternatives:

Assez	Quite	*Un peu*	A bit
Vraiment	Really	*Extrêmement*	Extremely
Trop	Too	*Tellement*	Too

c) Use interesting adverbs

Mal	Badly	*Bien*	Well
Stupidement	Stupidly	*Malheureusement*	Unfortunately
Soudainement	Suddenly	*Franchement*	Frankly
Bizarrement	Bizarrely	*Doucement*	Gently

d) Pronouns

Pronouns help us to avoid repetition and score highly at GCSE.

Instead of *J'adore aller <u>à la gym</u>, je vais souvent <u>à la gym</u>* …
… write *J'adore aller <u>à la gym</u>, j'**y** vais souvent.*

Y replaces *à la gym* and means 'there'.

*As-tu des crayons? J'**en** ai besoin.*
Do you have any pencils? I need **some**.

*J'ai vu Sophie aujourd'hui, je vais **chez elle** ce soir.*
I saw Sophie today, I'm going to **her house** tonight.

e) Comparatives and Superlatives

Compare things by saying something is <u>more</u> … than something or <u>less</u> … than something. Note the agreements that go with these comparatives and superlatives.

   ✓ plus (adjective) que   more … than

*Le sport est **plus** exigeant **que** les maths.*
Sport is more demanding than maths.

✓ moins (adjective) que   less … than

*La géographie est **moins** stimulante **que** la chimie.*
Geography is less stimulating than chemistry.

✓ aussi (adjective) que   as … as

*L'allemand est **aussi** important **que** l'espagnol.*
German is as important as Spanish.

Whereas a **comparative** is better/bigger/smaller/worse etc than something, a **superlative** is the biggest/best/worst/least etc.

✓ le/la plus   the most

*Le théâtre est **la** matière **la plus** créative.*
Theatre is the most creative subject.

✓ le/la moins (adjective and agreement)

*Le dessin est **la** matière **la moins** fatigante.*
Art is the least tiring subject.

✓ meilleur que   better than

<u>La</u> musique est meilleure que l'anglais.
Music is better than English.

✓ le/la meilleur(e)   the best

*Le français est **la meilleure** matière.*
French is the best subject.

f) The present participle

✓ **En + present participle**

En jouant au tennis.   While playing tennis.
En regardant la télé.   While watching the television.
En allant en ville.   While going into town.

g) *Qui* and *Que*

✓ ***Qui* replaces nouns that are the subject of the verb**

*J'ai un pantalon **qui** est gris.*
I have some trousers, which are grey.

✓ *Que* **replaces nouns that are the object of the verb.**

J'ai la chemise que j'ai achetée hier.
I have the shirt **that** I bought yesterday.

h) *Où*

✓ *Où* **replaces places**

J'ai vu l'hôtel où je suis resté pendant mes vacances.
I saw the hotel where I stayed on holiday.

i) Negative expressions

ne…personne	*nobody*
ne…rien	*not any*
ne…pas	*not*
ne…jamais	*never*
ne…que	*only*

*Don't forget that in this type of expression, *du, de la, de l'* and *des* all change to *de*, e.g.

Je n'ai pas de livres.
I don't have any books.

j) Subjunctive

The subjunctive isn't strictly a GCSE structure but you can **learn a set phrase to include in your work,** as it will get you extra marks. The subjunctive is used to express hypothetical things or wishes, opinions, and doubts. It is also used after these constructions:

Il faut que j'aille…	I have to go…
Il faut que je fasse…	I have to do…
Bien que ce soit…	Although it is…

E.g. *Bien que ce soit une matière difficile, j'aime l'histoire parce qu'elle est utile.*
Although it's a difficult subject, I like history because it is useful.

7. Dos and Don'ts

Do
- ✓ prepare a sentence for good weather, e.g. *il faisait beau*.
- ✓ prepare a sentence for bad weather, e.g. *il fait orageux*.
- ✓ prepare a sentence for what you ate, e.g. *j'ai bien mange*.
- ✓ use a positive concluding sentence, e.g. *Je me suis très bien amusé …*
- ✓ … or use a negative concluding sentence, e.g. *Nous ne nous sommes pas bien amusés*.
- ✓ plan out your essay.
- ✓ respect the word limit.
- ✓ leave five minutes to check for mistakes.
- ✓ write in the correct tense.
- ✓ answer the question fully.
- ✓ revise vocab, vocab, vocab!

Don't
- ✘ make things too complicated.
- ✘ miss out accents or try and make them flat!
- ✘ miss out punctuation.
- ✘ use google translate or equivalent websites for your homework, as they are not accurate enough.

Avoiding Common Mistakes

- ➤ *Les vacances* is always plural.

- ➤ *Comment* means 'how' **and** 'what':
  - o *Comment ça-va?*   How are you?
  - o *Comment est ta chambre?*   What's your room like?

- ➤ Spelling of *bea**U**coup*.

- ➤ 'At the weekend' is *le weekend* (not *sur le weekend*).

- ➤ Abbreviate *que* if it is followed by a vowel: *parce qu'il*.

- ➤ Note the differences between these similar words:
  - o *à* – to   *a* – has (*il a*)
  - o *où* – where   *ou* – or
  - o *et* – and   *est* – is (*il est*)

- ➤ If you have started with *tu* or *vous* then make sure you stick with your choice.

ONE MONTHLY FEE
NO PAYMENT CONTRACT

11 Plus Lifeline is the all-round solution for your child's 11+ preparation. It's also perfect for any child who wants an engaging, enjoyable way to reinforce their Key Stage 2 knowledge.

- Challenging, original practice papers to download and print.
- Fully worked example answers for every question, with step-by-step explanations: like expert private tuition.
- Suitable for independent and grammar schools.
- English Comprehension, Maths, Creative & Persuasive Writing, Reasoning (VR & NVR) and bonus material.
- Written and multiple-choice formats.
- Solutions to real past papers from leading schools – with example answers, discussions and full working.
- Individual marking and feedback available for your child's work.
- Cancel at any time.
- Ideal for children in Years 5 & 6.

"I passed the exam, most of which was because of your help! I don't have an actual tutor like most of my friends, but I feel so lucky to have your papers every week. I think you are the best tutor!" - David Tao, 11

WWW.11PLUSLIFELINE.COM

BV - #0018 - 110422 - C6 - 297/210/7 - PB - 9781914127106 - Gloss Lamination